ACKNOWLEDGEMENTS

As mentioned above, photographs of Canterbury from the late 1940s are quite hard to find, so I am especially grateful to the following for contributing them: Alan Stingemore, Rob Williams, Ted Yeoman, Invicta Motors Ltd, The Canterbury Archaeological Trust, Canterbury Museums and Messenger Group Newspapers. All photographs used are individually credited to the photographer and/or the contributor.

I would also like to thank Gerry Whittaker for the excellent photographic printing and individually, Ken Reedie, Tom Hodgson and Brian Stewart of the Canterbury Museums for their continued support and assistance. Finally, thanks must once again go to Anthony Swaine, architect, conservationist and lover of old Canterbury.

In the photo captions, cross referencing back to previous volumes has once again been included viz: The Blitz of Canterbury (BOC), Canterbury Then And Now (TAN), Canterbury Before the Blitz , (CBB) and Canterbury After the Blitz (CAB).

The Feature 'Canterbury Then And Now' appears regularly in the Kentish Gazette.

The author   (Photograph by Margaret Presdee)

This wonderful 1946 view perfectly captures the atmosphere of late 1940s Canterbury. The photographer is looking across St George's Lane and over the wastelands of the St George's parish. The mutilated church of that parish stands defiantly in a sea of vegetation, its future then uncertain. As can all too clearly be seen, the blitz and the merciless demolition and clearance afterwards opened up an unobstructed view of the Cathedral, a short lived delight unique to Canterbury in the late 1940s.

(Fisk-Moore)

THE OLD LONDON ROAD

This wonderful rural scene was captured in 1949, in an age before the motor car was master. This would have been the first close view of the Cathedral the pilgrims to Canterbury would have had, as they passed through Harbledown and down Summer Hill, near journey's end.

At the bottom of Summer Hill the road curves gently to the left and becomes London Road. At this point Mill Lane veers off sharply to the right, to serve a few houses and cottages. This junction also marks the line of the city boundary. Everything beyond it is officially in the City of Canterbury.

Between Summer Hill and the edge of the city can be seen the fields and water meadows stretching down to the River Stour, an area often captured by 19th century Canterbury artist, Thomas Sydney Cooper.

In the late 1940s traffic was not that heavy along this stretch of the old A2, but at times it was enough to cause a problem when it joined with the Whitstable traffic into St Dunstan's Street. Therefore, to avoid the bottlenecks of the railway crossing, Westgate Towers and the Kingsbridge, the post war Holden Plan of 1945 included an A2 diversion road that would take A2 traffic straight onto the planned ring road. The later Wilson Plan of 1947, implemented in 1951, also included an A2 diversion road that, as traffic built up throughout the 1950s, became increasingly more necessary.

The A2 diversion road was destined to go through the fields seen in the old picture and indeed it did, as the current picture testifies. Named the Rheims Way, the new road was opened in 1963.

(Fisk-Moore)

London Road roundabout, visible in the foreground, was not constructed at the same time as the Rheims Way. Originally, the road intersection was built as a crossroads, but this proved to be too hazardous for both cars and pedestrians. The Harbledown by-pass in the immediate foreground is a much more recent addition to the local road network.

Today, the view of the Cathedral from this vantage point is still impressive. In fact, motorists can enjoy a lingering look as they drive into Canterbury along the Rheims Way.

(Paul Crampton)

The accompanying photograph features the village of Harbledown on a fine summer's day, sometime in the late 1940s. The Fisk-Moore photographer has captured a scene completely devoid of all traffic, a reasonably rare occurrence even in this era considering that this was the main A2 road from London.

Lanfranc's Church of St Nicholas can be seen in its commanding position atop the hill on the right. Originally built as part of a leper hospital, it is now surrounded by early Victorian almshouses.

Harbledown's traffic problem worsened throughout the 1950s and 1960s. The introduction of articulated lorries, plying to and from the continent, exacerbated the situation. Villages such as Harbledown, Boughton and Bridge had to suffer from not only the noise and pollution, but also the many nasty accidents involving these gigantic vehicles.

(Fisk-Moore)

This is a scene that could never be captured today, London Road completely devoid of traffic, either moving or parked. The photographer even felt confident enough to set up his tripod in the middle of the road. He is looking towards the St Dunstan's end of London Road, where some ancient white rendered cottages can just be seen.

To the left of the picture can be seen the junction of Temple Road that led into a small estate of pre-fabricated houses, or pre-fabs. Sadly, I have not been able to locate a photograph of these at this time.

Most of the houses in London Road are large detached properties built in the Victorian period, although today many have become hotels or guest houses. However, older properties can be found at the St Dunstan's end of the road, including some fine examples of straightforward late Georgian and Regency architecture.

(Fisk-Moore)

This picture dates from 1947 and was taken by Rob Williams from Whitehall Bridge Road. His colleague Geoff Fuller is making a cine film of the same subject, the Cathedral, visible through a convenient gap in the trees of Westgate Gardens.

At this time Whitehall Bridge Road was no more than a tiny winding lane that linked the end of Orchard Street with Whitehall Road. The latter named road can be seen in the middle distance, running alongside the wall of Westgate Gardens. Had the Holden Plan been implemented, then the ring road would have replaced Whitehall Road at this location. Holden's roundabout, connecting the A2 diversion road with the ring road, would have been situated just to the right of the present junction with Whitehall Bridge Road. Wilson's ring road was destined to pass by on the other side of Westgate Gardens and the River Stour, along the line of St Peter's Place.

(Rob Williams)

THE WESTGATE AREA

This wonderful cityscape was taken from the top of the Westgate in about 1949 or 1950. It clearly shows just how much of the western end of the main street had survived the blitz. The only casualty was Barrett's Garage in St Peter's Street, seen in the foreground on the left. The empty site closest to the camera was once occupied by a lofty timber framed building that was burnt to the ground in January 1944. Charred timbers from it still survive, embedded in the party wall of the next brick building that was itself damaged in the same raid.

A post-war Dennis single deck bus can be seen going up St Peter's Street and is about to meet a Leyland double decker coming in the opposite direction.

On the right is the Seeboard showroom, in the building once occupied by the Corner House Café. Beyond it is another white rendered building,

F.G. Cornfoot the Chemists. Just out of sight on the right is the East Kent Bus Station in St Peter's Place. All of the above mentioned buildings were threatened by post-war road plans. The Holden Plan of 1945 envisaged a long rectangular roundabout across the Barrett's site, where traffic from the extra-mural ring road and the cross-city relief road would meet. This plan was subsequently dropped. The replacement Wilson road plan of 1947 brought the ring road inside the city wall at this point, to pass across the area in the foreground of the picture.

The latter plan was adopted in 1951. This, of course, prevented Barretts from rebuilding their premises on the same site. All the affected buildings were demolished around 10 years later.
See CBB, Page 4 and CAB, Page 3 – Bottom (Fisk-Moore)

Sadly, the buildings at this end of St Peter's Street were demolished for nothing, as the ring road never came through here. Plans to complete the ring road circuit were scrapped in 1975. Barretts were then free, at long last, to extend their premises. The new buildings are visible in the foreground. There was also a planning application to rebuild the corner house on its original site. This idea would appear to have come to nothing. The rest of St Peter's Street has changed very little, although the shops opposite the Kentish Cricketers are of post-war construction.

(Paul Crampton)

This photograph was taken from the same vantage point as the ones on the opposite page. It shows a carnival or festival parade passing along St Peter's Street in the late 1940s. The St Peter's Street section of the main thoroughfare was reasonably wide, but it narrowed considerably when passing over Kingsbridge. This was a major factor in the decision taken by Holden and Wilson to provide a relief road parallel to the existing main street.

Under the Holden Plan, a one-way traffic flow system was envisaged, with traffic running east to west on the new relief road and west to east on the existing main street. The Wilson Plan proposed that traffic travel in both directions on both streets. However, his version of the relief road was designed to take the bulk of the traffic, including buses. The Wilson relief road was begun, including much preliminary demolition, but was never completed.

(Bill Entwistle)

The photographer also captured the same parade in the other direction as it proceeded along St Dunstan's Street. Many fine ancient timber framed buildings can be seen on both sides of the street in this late 1940s view. Fortunately, they all survive today, but that would not be the case had the Holden Plan been implemented. Holden's ring road bisected St Dunstan's Street just beyond the Falstaff Inn, the projecting sign of which can just be seen on the right. The Falstaff and all the old buildings on both sides of the street, between the Westgate and the proposed ring road, were to be retained. However, everything else beyond the Falstaff on the right hand side of the street was to be demolished, including the medieval George And Dragon Inn (now The Bishop's Finger). This was to make way for not only the ring road, but also an open square. Buildings on the left hand side of the street fared better, apart from the large gap needed for the ring road. At least the multi-gabled 16th century buildings furthest from the camera on the left were to be retained.

See CBB, Page 3 – Middle (Bill Entwistle)

A wonderful 1948 view of St Dunstan's Street, looking back towards the Westgate. At this time, through traffic from both the A2 London Road and Whitstable Road passed along here. It all had to encounter the Westgate Towers bottleneck and St Dunstan's Street level crossing, both of which could slow traffic considerably. This goes a long way to explain why an A2 diversion road featured in both Holden and Wilson Plans. However, Fisk-Moore has chosen another quiet day for his picture!

By the time this photograph was taken, the Holden proposals, as described in the above caption, had long since been forgotten. The replacement Wilson Plan left St Dunstan's Street alone and moved the proposed ring road to the St Peter's Street side of the Westgate. The buildings in St Dunstan's Street look very much as they do today. Only the people and traffic have changed. Now, there are a lot more of each.

See CBB, Page 3 – Bottom (Fisk-Moore)

THE FRIARS

Tall buildings in Canterbury have always proved to be good vantage points from which to photograph the Cathedral. The Westgate, the Findon Gate and Abbotts Mill were all favourites. When the last mentioned burned down in 1933 photographers used the Friars Cinema instead, which had been built in the same year.

This particular view was taken in 1946 and shows an interesting group of buildings around the crossroads where meet The Friars, King Street, Orange Street and Best Lane. Just below the centre of the picture is an empty site where some wooden buildings had once stood, but had become victims of the blitz. On the other side of the site can be seen a damaged three-storey building with a tiled rear elevation (No. 2 Best Lane). A very similar house once adjoined it on the left, but this too was a blitz casualty. Another interesting building of note is the shop standing on the corner of Orange Street and King Street. This is the premises of Glutenia Foods Co., diabetic products, at No. 8 Orange Street. It was a late medieval timber framed structure with a much later façade that hid the building's true antiquity.

The Wilson Road Plan of 1947 showed Best Lane and King Street widened to form part of the main internal street framework. Consequently, from the late 1940s onwards, a number of buildings on either side of both streets were demolished. Both individual buildings mentioned above no longer exist and may have been victims of this process.

In the foreground can be seen a row of small warehouses, standing along the edge of the River Stour. Many of these were dismantled from 1947 onwards.

(Fisk-Moore)

The Art Deco façade of the old Friars Cinema, from which the old photograph was taken, still survives and was incorporated into the present Marlowe Theatre. This enabled me to take the current view from the same vantage point. In fact, views across the Canterbury rooftops from this high position look superb in any direction. The empty site in The Friars, visible in both pictures, may soon be redeveloped. I am grateful to Peter Walker of the Marlowe Theatre for access and permission to take the current photograph.

(Paul Crampton)

This picture dates from 1949 and was taken from a small piece of open land to the north of The Friars. The River Stour flows by unseen in the middle distance, just behind the trees. Earlier in the same decade, this plot was occupied by Friars Garage Ltd, being situated behind their main building on the street frontage. By 1949 that building, at Nos. 4 and 5 The Friars, had been converted to the San Maria Restaurant. The minor garage buildings to the rear had been demolished and the area just laid out as a garden when the photograph was taken.

The buildings seen on the right of this view are on the north side of The Friars and can be seen to the left of the old picture on the opposite page. Buildings situated in King Street are visible between the trees.

Today the building once occupied by the restaurant has reverted to being a garage showroom. The garden area is now a parking lot for selling cars.

(Fisk-Moore)

This lovely late 1940s view was taken from Friars Bridge and looks north along the River Stour. The old Blackfriars Refectory building is casting a clear reflection in the calm waters of the river. At this time it was being used by the First Church of Christ Scientist.

The large empty site on the right was once occupied by Green and Company, the Fellmongers. For many years their lofty premises obscured views of the old friary building, but no more. The lower parts of the wall of the demolished riverside building can still be seen. A boat of the Blackfriars River Tours waits in vain for some passengers. Today river tour boats can be picked up from the same point.

To the right can be seen the chimneys of the houses, as well as a large warehouse situated in Blackfriars Street. The houses still exist, but the warehouse opposite them has gone.

See CBB, Page 8

(Fisk-Moore)

Another superb cityscape taken from the old Friars Cinema. This particular view dates from 1947 and was taken almost exactly one year after the large picture on the opposite page. Although only a short period of time separates the two views, close examination reveals that a number of changes have already taken place. The old building at No. 8 Orange Street, as described opposite, now seems to be empty and more derelict in appearance. The exact date of its demolition is not known, but it had certainly gone by the mid 1950s. Another change is the removal of the old pitched roof of one of the riverside warehouses, replaced by one of a single pitch, constructed in corrugated iron.

The most obvious change is to the Cathedral, as by 1947 the scaffolding had been removed from the south-west pinnacle of Bell Harry Tower. This had been in place throughout the war years and is prominent in blitz period views of the Cathedral.

(Fisk-Moore)

THE SITE OF ALL SAINTS' CHURCH

There is a certain amount of confusion concerning All Saints' Church in Canterbury. I have heard conflicting reports about its history, its fate and even its location. Moreover, there are many people in Canterbury who have never heard of it at all.

All Saints' was a Regency church, built of yellow bricks in 1828. It stood on the corner of Best Lane and the High Street, opposite the main post office near Kingsbridge. It had replaced a medieval church on the same site. All Saints' was made redundant when its parish amalgamated with that of St Alphege. It became All Saints' Hall for a period, then was eventually demolished in 1937 or 1938. Therefore, it was not a blitz victim, nor a casualty of post-war road widening.

The old photograph was taken in 1948, when the site had been empty for ten years, except for air raid shelters that were erected here at the beginning of the last war. The west wall of the church was not demolished and can be seen abutted against the next building. The trenches across the site are a mystery as they do not appear to relate to any known archaeological investigation. It is also unlikely to be the start of the redevelopment of the site, as construction of the new gas showrooms did not begin until 1952.

Today much evidence of the existence of All Saints' Church can be found. The outline of the medieval church has been marked out in the pavement and the tiny churchyard in Best Lane still exists. Moreover, in a dark corner of the churchyard, there can be seen a fragment of flint wall, which may have been part of the older church.   (Fisk-Moore)

The new gas showroom building was completed in 1953. It was constructed well back from the existing Best Lane frontage, to allow for later road widening in accordance with the development plan (see page 6). The original Regency period churchyard wall still survived in Best Lane throughout most of the 1950s. It was later removed, but has recently been rebuilt to enclose the old churchyard once more. The 1953 building (no longer the gas showroom) is a handsome structure and one of the better examples of 1950s architecture in Canterbury.

(Paul Crampton)

Virtually opposite the site of All Saints' Church can be found the ancient Eastbridge Hospital, dedicated to St Thomas the Martyr. It was founded in 1180, only ten years after the martyrdom, and has been much altered over the centuries. Canterbury's main street narrows considerably at this point, due to the angled siting of the Eastbridge Hospital and the narrowness of the King's Bridge (or East Bridge) over the River Stour. Partly to overcome this problem, the Holden Plan of 1945 included the parallel relief road that crossed the Stour just behind the Eastbridge Hospital. The rival plan, proposed by the CCDA, did not include a parallel road. However, they had an almost equally bizarre proposal to alleviate the Kingsbridge bottleneck. They wanted not only to widen the existing Kingsbridge, but also to demolish the front elevation of Eastbridge Hospital and rebuild it further back. I cannot imagine what the conservationist lobby within the CCDA thought of this idea!
See CBB, Page 15 – Bottom Right (Fisk-Moore)

This picture dates from 1949 and was taken in the opposite direction to the one above, with Kingsbridge behind the cameraman. The former site of All Saints' Church is on the left of this view, behind the tree and fence. East Kent buses are much in evidence. The single-deck Dennis Lancet bus probably had to wait for the double-deckers to pass, before it could proceed over Kingsbridge. The 1945 CCDA alternative development plan, mentioned above, was forgotten along with the Holden Plan, following the November 1945 local elections. In 1946 the victorious CCDA-nominated council attempted to come up with a new plan, effectively a compromise between the two plans from 1945. To solve the Kingsbridge problem they proposed a short loop road just to the north, linking Best Lane with The Friars and bisecting All Saints' Lane on the way. This idea was proved unworkable and, in 1947, the Wilson Plan re-introduced the parallel road idea. However, Wilson's relief road was further south than Holden's at this location. (Alan Stingemore)

On the other side of Kingsbridge and just into St Peter's Street is one of the most mysterious and seldom seen old houses in Canterbury. Hidden behind a high brick wall on the south side of the street is the Master's Lodge to Eastbridge Hospital. This is largely a 14th century timber framed house with alterations from the 16th, 17th and 18th centuries. However, what can be seen in the accompanying photographs is the Victorian north wing extension to the Lodge House. This was constructed of brick and medieval demolition material, no doubt recovered from nearby ruinous monastic buildings, such as Greyfriars. During later restoration work, local architect Anthony Swaine completely removed this Victorian addition and once more revealed the original timber framed façade. He also carried out extensive restoration work at Eastbridge Hospital itself and was responsible for the removal of the Victorian crenellations to the flint façade. The two pictures on the opposite page show the effect of this restoration work.

(Bill Entwistle)

STOUR STREET

Stour Street was well away from the main area of Canterbury affected by the 1942 blitz. Although only one high explosive bomb fell on the street, that one bomb badly damaged all the buildings situated around the Stour Street, Beer Cart Lane junction. All but one of the affected buildings were demolished in the weeks after the blitz. The one exception was the 14th century Poor Priests Hospital. This building required extensive repairs to the roof caused by severe blast, but was otherwise in reasonable condition.

The Poor Priests Hospital is pictured here in about 1946. At this time the former medieval hospital housed the headquarters of the St John Ambulance Brigade, the medical comfort depot of the St John Ambulance Association and the Canterbury Health Department. Parked outside is one of the large left hand drive field ambulances, donated by the Canadian Government at the beginning of the 1940s.

The 1945 Holden Plan proposed that one of its typical elongated roundabouts (effectively, an open space with roadway on all sides) be constructed on the empty bombsite opposite the Poor Priests. This would handle traffic from Stour Street, Beer Cart Lane and Hawks Lane. However, the Holden version of the cross city relief road was well away from this area, and crossed Stour Street near to the telephone exchange further down.

The 1947 Wilson Plan brought the relief road very much closer and showed it passing just to the north of the Poor Priests. The white jettied building seen on the right would have been in its path. Stour Street was also shown as forming an integral part of the internal street framework that would have necessitated its widening and straightening. However, by 1951, when the Wilson Plan was implemented, the latter idea had been temporarily shelved.

See CAB, Page 7 – Bottom　　　　　　　　　　　　　　　　(Fisk-Moore)

Stour Street was the subject of road improvement plans right up until the early 1970s. The last proposal had Stour Street widened to become an access road to a lorry unloading area just off Jewry Lane. Known unofficially as the 'Stour Street motorway', this plan was scrapped in favour of restoring the street to residential use. The Poor Priests Hospital has also undergone changes over the years. Restoration work has removed a number of post-medieval additions to the original fabric, including dormer windows and some chimney stacks.

(Paul Crampton)

This lovely photograph dates from the summer of 1946 and shows the old dormitory building that once formed part of the Greyfriars Franciscan friary. The friary precincts, once totalling some 18 acres, could be found behind the Poor Priests Hospital on the other side of the River Stour. The dormitory is the only surviving building of the Greyfriars, although fragments of the church, probably the west wall of the chancel, can be found just to the north. After the dissolution, parts of the friary, including the former dormitory, became a private dwelling. Some fine red bricked garden walls survive from this period. Part of a wall and gateway (re-using medieval stonework) can be seen in the gap on the right, behind the Laburnum and Beech trees. Recently, the gateway subsided and was in danger of collapse. Whilst excavating in an effort to strengthen its foundations, the south-east corner of the old Greyfriars Church was discovered.

(Fisk-Moore)

This picture was taken in the opposite direction to the one on page 10. The Salvation Army parade has just turned into Stour Street from Beer Cart Lane and are about to march past the Poor Priests Hospital, behind the camera.

In the background is a group of industrial buildings that were once part of a large brewery complex run by Rigden and Company. By the late 1940s local hauliers C. & C. Yeoman were using some of these buildings for storage. This area was outside the 75-acre compulsory purchase area, under the first stage development of the Holden Plan. The replacement Wilson Plan, as it was first conceived, included a north–south relief road. This was a widening of existing roads, including Stour Street, Best Lane and King Street, rather than a new road like the planned east–west relief road. A vast roundabout was planned at the intersection of the two roads. This was to be sited on Stour Street, between the junctions of Hawks Lane and Jewry Lane.
See TAN, Page 1 (Courtesy Canterbury Museums)

St Edmund's Road is a short cul de sac that comes off the west side of Stour Street and runs down to the river. In the accompanying picture the photographer is standing with his back to the Stour and is looking up towards Stour Street and Hospital Lane beyond. Mid-Victorian terraced houses can be seen on either side. It is interesting to note that at this time the road was unmetalled!

Neither the first stage Holden Plan nor the Wilson Plan involved St Edmund's Road in any way, although the proposed widening of Stour Street under the latter may have affected the cornershop (unseen here) at the top of the road. St Edmund's Road was finally metalled in the late 1950s and sometime after that the gap in the middle on the right was developed with houses.

(Fisk-Moore)

WINCHEAP

In the late 1940s, well away from the blitzed area of the city, things carried on as normal, very much as they had before the bombing. The area around Wincheap Green was not affected by the blitz, but would be changed radically by the coming of the ring road in the early 1960s.

The accompanying photograph was taken long before the construction of the ring road, but at a time when it was being planned. It shows two fine 18th century houses that stood at the point where Castle Street became Wincheap. The larger house on the right dates from the mid 18th century and represents a type still be to found in Canterbury today. It was known as 'The Cedars' and at this time was the office premises of local road contractors and hauliers C. & G. Yeoman.

The house on the left, at No. 1 Wincheap, was also in the ownership of the Yeoman family, but as a private residence. It dates from the late

18th century and is built in a sort of transitional Georgian-Regency style. The stuccoed façade may have hidden a much older timber framed structure, but this is by no means certain. The adjacent house at No. 2 Wincheap (out of sight to the left) was indeed timber framed and dated from the late 16th or early 17th centuries.

C. & G. Yeoman were well known in Canterbury and had more premises in Beer Cart Lane and further along Wincheap, where the Exhaust Centre is now. Upon Nationalisation in 1949, Yeomans became part of the British Road Services, who remained in the larger of the two Georgian houses and in the depot to its rear, until the coming of the ring road in 1963.

See TAN, Page 3 – Bottom   (Ted Yeoman)

The houses in the photograph were amongst the last properties to be demolished, just prior to completion of the first stage of the ring road in 1963. They stood while much of the Rheims Way was being constructed and only came down when Wincheap roundabout was built. This then linked the new road in with the existing road system. British Road Services continued to be based at this location, albeit on a slightly reduced site. A new office building also appeared, just off nearby St Andrew's Close. Today Habitat has replaced the old BRS depot.

(Paul Crampton)

This photograph, taken from Wincheap Green, shows the buildings on the corner of Worthgate Place to the left, with Pin Hill to the right. The building nearest the camera is the Man of Kent public house. It incorporated a pair of 17th century cottages (fronting Worthgate Place) and a 19th century slate roofed extension. Both Holden and Wilson Plans showed the ring road passing through this area, so the pub and the Edwardian houses further along Pin Hill were blighted from 1945 onwards. However, in 1969 when the ring road was extended, the 17th century part of the pub was saved and can be seen today.

(Messenger Group Newspapers)

Simmonds Row was a short street running westwards off Wincheap Street, near the Maiden's Head public house. It contained two rows of tiny 18th or early 19th century brick built cottages. When this 1940s photograph was taken, the row on the left (Nos. 1 to 9) were mostly empty and awaiting demolition. They finally came down in the early 1950s. The right hand row at Nos. 10 to 17 Simmonds Row survived until about 1968, when they were pulled down in advance of the creation of the Wincheap Industrial Estate. The street was then widened and renamed Simmonds Road.

(Messenger Group Newspapers)

This fascinating picture dates from 1949 and shows the limeworks and quarry of Frank Cooper Ltd, situated at the end of the appropriately-named Lime Kiln Road in Wincheap. This view looks north and back towards central Canterbury. The processing shed can be seen on the left and two kilns are just visible in the distance on the right. The Elham Valley Line crosses the site in the middle distance. The limeworks closed in the early 1960s and most of the buildings were demolished in September 1965. The overgrown and partly filled quarry can still be seen today.

(Fisk-Moore)

High Street has lost some significant buildings in the 44 years that separate the 'then and now' views. The Guildhall gradually disappeared between 1949 and 1955, followed by the medieval Fleur De Lys Hotel and the Regency entrance building to Foresters Hall in the late 1950s. Lastly, Baldwins shop, that encompassed two late medieval structures, was demolished in the early 1970s. Of the remaining buildings, including those in the current view, only the shop fronts and traders have changed. It is sad to reflect that in the High Street today there are no general grocers' shops left.

HIGH STREET

The entire length of Canterbury's main shopping thoroughfare is often referred to as the High Street. In fact only the section from Mercery Lane to Kingsbridge is actually called 'High Street'. In the late 1940s, with the prestigious end of the main street, St George's Street, all but gone, it was to the High Street that most of the shoppers now flocked.

The accompanying photograph, taken by Alan Stingemore, shows a busy scene on the north side of the High Street in 1949. The old Guildhall is just visible on the right. The first shop on the right is the premises of Currys Ltd at No. 12 High Street. This is a 15th century timber framed building with 17th and 19th century alterations. The poor condition of the adjacent Guildhall was also having an adverse effect on the Currys' premises. The front two bays of the party wall between Currys and the Guildhall was timber framed and badly infected by Death Watch Beetle. This was covered with two layers of crumbling lath and plaster. The rest of the party wall was of more substantial flint and chalk block construction, but this had been hacked back at various locations, weakening the structure. The problem was so severe that the party wall had to be shored up from inside the Currys' shop.

The problem was resolved, at least for Currys, by the demolition of much of the Guildhall from 1949 onwards. This was followed by the construction of a new fire resistant wall between Currys and the now vacant site.

Returning to the old picture, the middle shop is the Maypole Dairy Co., grocers' at 13 High Street. The building's history is the same as that for the Currys' premises. On the left is another grocer's shop, that of Lipton Ltd at No. 14.

(Alan Stingemore)

The right hand photograph dates from the mid 1940s and features on the left of the view the narrow entrance building into the Foresters Hall. This is a Regency building that was constructed in a gap between two then existing structures. One of these is the Georgian shop prominent in the picture, the other was the church of St Mary Bredman. This church was demolished in 1900, but its west wall survived, abutted against the Foresters Hall entrance building. The south wall of the church also survived at this time and still incorporated a medieval door and window. Behind the narrow entrance building was the hall proper. This was an ancient timber framed structure that had once been called Church House. In the late 1940s Foresters Hall housed a number of businesses and associations, including the Woodman School of Dancing, Bill Entwistle photographer, the Home Guard Association and the Ancient Order of Foresters.

(Photograph © RCHM)

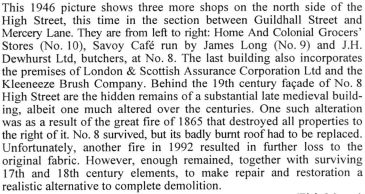

This 1946 picture shows three more shops on the north side of the High Street, this time in the section between Guildhall Street and Mercery Lane. They are from left to right: Home And Colonial Grocers' Stores (No. 10), Savoy Café run by James Long (No. 9) and J.H. Dewhurst Ltd, butchers, at No. 8. The last building also incorporates the premises of London & Scottish Assurance Corporation Ltd and the Kleeneeze Brush Company. Behind the 19th century façade of No. 8 High Street are the hidden remains of a substantial late medieval building, albeit one much altered over the centuries. One such alteration was as a result of the great fire of 1865 that destroyed all properties to the right of it. No. 8 survived, but its badly burnt roof had to be replaced. Unfortunately, another fire in 1992 resulted in further loss to the original fabric. However, enough remained, together with surviving 17th and 18th century elements, to make repair and restoration a realistic alternative to complete demolition.

(Fisk-Moore)

Another 1949 view of the High Street from the camera of Alan Stingemore, taken at the same time as the one on the opposite page. This photograph includes a much better view of Lipton Ltd, grocers, at No. 14 High Street. To the left is the public house The Bell Hotel (No. 15), which at this time had Mrs D.E. Callender listed as publican. The pub hoarding advertises George Beer and Rigdens Ales, but it later became a Fremlins House. Further left still and just visible are the premises of Clement Clarke Ltd, dispensing opticians, at No. 16 High Street.

In the late 1940s Canterbury's main street contained many useful shops, even allowing for the fact that St George's Street was all but gone. The High Street section alone contained nine separate grocers or foodstores. Sadly, they have all disappeared over the intervening years. Also now only a memory is The Bell Hotel that closed for good in 1974.

(Alan Stingemore)

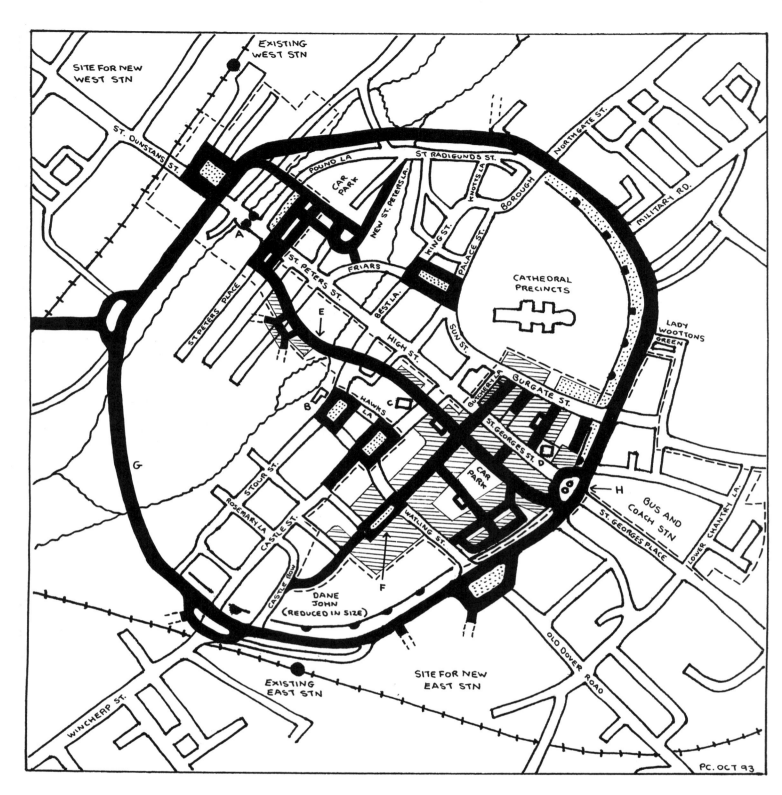

HOLDEN PLAN - 1945 (First stage development)

Compulsory purchase requirement — 75 acres (area ---)

☐ :	Existing roads unchanged.
▬ :	New roads (or existing roads widened).
▨ :	New buildings (First stage only).
▦ :	New open spaces.
▬ --- :	New roads for later stages.

Points of Reference :

A - Westgate.   B - Poor Priests Hospital.
C - St Margarets Ch.   D - St Georges Ch.
E — East-West relief road. (Single Carriageway).
F — Civic Way. (Dual Carriageway)
G — Extra mural ring road. (ie. all outside line of city wall).
H — Remains of St Georges City Gate exposed.

THE 1945 HOLDEN PLAN

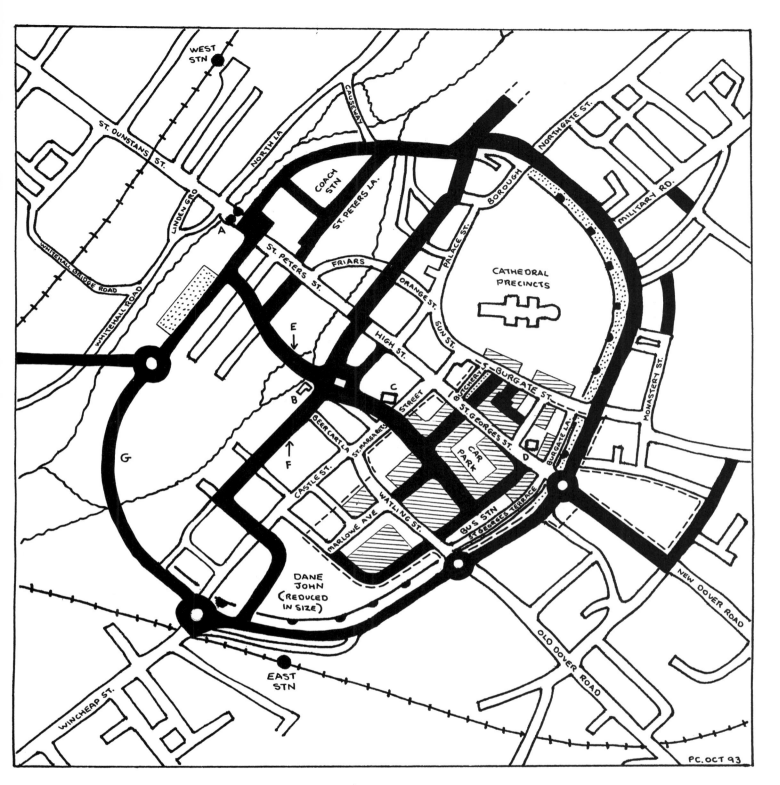

WILSON PLAN - 1947 (Town & Country Planning Act)

Compulsory purchase requirement — 33½ acres (area - - -)

Points of Reference:
A - Westgate. B - Poor Priests Hospital.
C - St Margarets Ch. D - St Georges Ch.

E - East-West relief road. (Dual Carriageway).

F - North-South relief road. (Existing roads widened).

G - Intra and Extra mural ring road.

☐ : Existing roads unchanged.

■ : New roads (or existing roads widened).

▨ : New buildings (Excluding slum clearance).

⊡ : New open spaces.

■-- : New roads for the future (Sturry radial).

THE 1947 WILSON PLAN

THE OLD GUILDHALL & GUILDHALL STREET

In the late 1940s the Guildhall was in a poor state of repair and a considerable amount of time and money would have been needed to prevent it from serious and perhaps irreversible deterioration. This is not disputed. The controversy comes from the ultimate decision made, that the standing fabric of the Guildhall (above ground level) was not sufficiently important nor historic enough to justify the expense.

Briefly, the Guildhall consisted of a Regency frontage to the High Street, built in 1835, and a poorly constructed neo-Regency Guildhall Street façade, probably Edwardian. At the heart of the building were surviving elements of a medieval timber frame and beneath, the remains of a Romanesque undercroft.

On several occasions in 1947 City Architect Hugh Wilson examined the fabric of the Guildhall, in the company of officers from the Ancient Monuments Department of the Ministry of Works. In July 1948 he submitted a full and frank report to the city council. This detailed the many problems with the Guildhall structure and also listed the proposed repairs needed to overcome them.

The Ministry of Works were in favour of repair and listed the Guildhall as an ancient monument. Hugh Wilson designed new external elevations for the building, whilst carrying out further and, necessarily, more invasive examinations of the structure.

By 1949 it was reported that to carry out proper repairs the Guildhall would need to be dismantled to within a few feet of the ground and then rebuilt. Much of the dangerous roof was removed at this time, as the 1949 picture shows. Town Clerk John Boyle argued that as the rebuilt Guildhall would contain very little ancient fabric, why rebuild it at all? In 1950 the demolition of most of the Guildhall above ground level was carried out and the Ministry of Works reluctantly accepted the Town Clerk's argument.

See CBB, Page 15 – Top and TAN, Pages 6 & 7 – Middle

(Courtesy Canterbury Museums)

Construction of the shoe shop building on the site of the old Guildhall was completed in 1956. The new shop was set back to create a much wider junction into Guildhall Street, so that larger vehicles had better access. Beneath ground level the remains of the Romanesque undercroft were protected from the invading foundations of the new building. At the time the current picture was taken (October 1993) the shoe shop was undergoing extensive refurbishment. A recent plan to build a facsimile of the old Guildhall on the same site has now been shelved indefinitely.

(Paul Crampton)

The decision to demolish the Guildhall is still a controversial one today as far as conservationists are concerned.

The accompanying photograph shows the interior of the doomed building in happier days. The date is 12th November 1947 and the occasion is the election of the Mayor of Canterbury. Even at this time, the condition of the fabric was beginning to cause concern to City Architect L. Hugh Wilson, who encountered problems when making an initial investigation. On 10th December 1947, following further thorough examinations of the structure, he reported some alarming findings to the council. His report stated that the flank wall on Guildhall Street was badly fractured near the south-east corner and also leaning out. He further stated that dry rot had affected the rafters. Each subsequent investigation found more problems until, eventually, the fateful decision to demolish was made.

See TAN, Page 7 – Top   (Fisk-Moore)

A superb view of the perpendicular towers of the Cathedral, as seen from the south-west in 1949. The cameraman is standing on the scaffolding against the Guildhall Street elevation of the old Guildhall, probably during the removal of the roof timbers. A partially demolished section of the Guildhall structure can just be seen in the bottom left hand corner of the photograph.

The picture affords a particularly clear view of the upper storeys of the buildings standing on the east side of Guildhall Street. They are part of the extensive department store complex of William Lefevre Ltd. The building to the left is a three storey steel framed structure, clad in white ceramic tiles and with leaded lights to the first and second floors. It was put up in 1927 and is typical of the period, but rare for Canterbury. This new department store building replaced Thomas Sidney Cooper's Theatre Royal that had previously stood on this site for less than 70 years.

(Alan Stingemore)

This photograph, also from 1949, shows buildings on the west side of Guildhall Street and near the junction with Orange Street. Sun Street is situated behind the camera with Palace Street to the right. Guildhall Street was created in 1805, so none of its buildings are older than this date. The shops in the accompanying picture were probably amongst the first to be built along this 'new' street. The corner building on the right is the premises of Jay Furnishing Stores at No. 1 Guildhall Street. To the left is Burniston & Co., the coal merchants at No. 2.

Guildhall Street was not directly affected by the first stage of the Holden Plan, but nearby Orange Street was. An open space was to be created by the removal of all the buildings along the north side of Orange Street (visible to the right of the picture). This was to create a tree-lined square that extended as far along as Turnagain Lane. It is surprising that this open square, with all the necessary demolition of intact buildings to create it, was included in the first development stage of this plan.

(Fisk-Moore)

In 1965 the then City Architect, John Berbiers, more clearly defined the line of the parallel road in this part of the city. This slightly reduced the impact on St Margaret's Street, so that only four of the old shops on the street's west side needed to go. Ultimately, the plan was scrapped and all the affected buildings saved. Although nearly half a century separates the two views on this page, very little appears to have changed at the north end of St Margaret's Street. However, today it certainly appears to attract a lot more people!

(Paul Crampton)

ST MARGARET'S STREET

The accompanying old photograph was taken in April 1948 and shows the north end of St Margaret's Street. This part of the street has not changed very much in the last 45 years, although the shop fronts and the traders are very different. The 1948 traders included Lewis Chiropodists (No. 19), The Pilgrims Tea House (No. 20) and Walpamur Co., Paint Manufacturers (No. 21), all to be seen on the right of the picture in the foreground. Opposite these are London Outfitters Ltd (No. 30), George Mount Florists (No. 29b) and North Sea Fish Company at No. 29a.

Changes to this end of St Margaret's Street would have gone far beyond just a change of traders, had the Holden Plan of 1945 been implemented. This plan envisaged a cross-city relief road running south of and roughly parallel to the existing main street. The relief road would have crossed St Margaret's Street just to the north of St Margaret's Church, at exactly the point seen in the foreground of the old photograph. All of the shops listed above would have been demolished to make way for it.

The 1945 plan was dropped and replaced by the 1947 Wilson Plan. This new plan also included a relief road, but it was now destined to pass to the south of St Margaret's Church, thus safeguarding all of the buildings in the photograph. However, the 1947 plan would have necessitated the removal of some of the ancient buildings situated between the church and Hawks Lane.

See CBB, Page 17 – Bottom   (Fisk-Moore)

Another picture from April 1948, showing further buildings at the north end of the street. It is dominated by the empty 19th century three storey building at Nos. 22 and 23. Formerly it was part of Finns Stores, but had been empty for some time when this photograph was taken. Also by this time much of the elaborate ground floor elevation had been removed, giving the building a rather top heavy appearance. The surviving column on the right gives some indication of what the intact façade once looked like.

Holden's parallel relief road passed immediately to the south of this building, which would have placed it on a busy junction, had that plan been implemented. In 1949 new occupants arrived. They were F.N. Nason, Hotel Furnishers, a local firm that would expand in later years. The shop to the left belongs to Vye & Son, the grocers, at No. 24 St Margaret's Street. This also used to be part of Finns Stores, but had been taken over by Vye & Son in the mid 1930s.

(Fisk-Moore)

The old photograph on the opposite page features shops threatened by the Holden parallel relief road. The picture reproduced above shows those threatened by the replacement Wilson relief road. Hugh Wilson's plan had re-routed this road along a more southerly trajectory, to reduce the number of old buildings needing to be demolished. The shop in the centre of the picture, next to the junction with Hawks Lane, is B.C. Blyth & Son, Wine Merchants, at No. 36 St Margaret's Street. This timber framed building dates from about 1770, which is quite late for this method of construction. To the right of it can be seen three older shop buildings on the street's west side, also threatened at this time by the relief road.

The photographer is standing with his back to the surviving half of the Freemasons Tavern. The lost half, a victim of the blitz, once extended along to where the rockery can be seen. The Freemasons Tavern was also threatened by the route of Wilson's relief road, the only building on the street's east side to be so.

(Fisk-Moore)

This fascinating late 1940s picture was taken from the 'new' car park in St Margaret's Street, at a point that would once have been in the rear courtyard of the Royal Fountain Hotel. Chestnut paling surrounds the exposed cellars of the blitzed hotel, situated against the east side of the street. The car park access road from St Margaret's Street follows the exact line of the central passage that once ran through the main hotel building to the rear courtyard. St Margaret's Church on the west side of the street dominates the photograph and was its intended subject. The Holden Plan relief road would have passed to the right of it, whereas Wilson's road would have passed to the left. Both roads would have been very destructive to buildings on the west side of St Margaret's Street, as mentioned above. However, the Wilson Plan relief road had less impact on the east side, as it would have mostly crossed the empty hotel site, seen in the picture.

(Courtesy Canterbury College of Art)

WATLING STREET

Watling Street took a real hammering in the raids of both June and October 1942. One of the victims was the Victorian non-conformist chapel that was gutted in a minor raid during the first week of June 1942, then flattened in the daylight raid of 31st October the same year.

The street was also to see some changes in the late 1940s. One change was the arrival of a new, but temporary, Congregational Church in 1949. It was built on the site of the blitzed chapel and pictured here with construction work just completed. The empty sites on either side of the new church once contained large houses that were badly damaged in the October 1942 raid and later demolished.

Another change occurred on the opposite side of the road at about the same time. This was the demolition of a row of properties at Nos.

38 to 42 Watling Street. They stood where the surface car park can now be found. Included amongst the victims of the demolition gangs was a public house, the Dane John Tavern. Sadly, I cannot trace a photograph of these buildings taken in the late 1940s.

In the accompanying picture there are some interesting buildings visible in the background. Beyond the church to the left can be seen the back of the Central Picture Theatre in St Margaret's Street. In 1950 it would receive a large rear extension and become the first Marlowe Theatre. Behind the church to the right is a large Regency house, then standing on the corner of Gravel Walk and Rose Lane.

See CBB, Page 19 – Bottom right and BOC, Page 28 – Top left

(Fisk-Moore)

The temporary Congregational Church was subsequently replaced by the present structure in the mid 1950s, although a row over funding held up its completion for many months. This attractive building, now the United Reformed Church, will probably be demolished when the Whitefriars redevelopment scheme is eventually begun. I have been told that the building is suffering from 'concrete cancer', but cannot confirm this. A new larger church will then be constructed in the Watling Street car park, opposite the present building.

(Paul Crampton)

This wonderful atmospheric scene was captured in early 1946. It looks through the Riding Gate and down Watling Street, where a number of blitz surviving buildings can be seen. In the foreground are some memories of Canterbury at war, including barbed wire and plane spotting posters. Scars of buildings destroyed in the 1942 raids can be seen against the city wall on the right.

The first building on the other side of the Riding Gate is No. 1 Watling Street, a large Georgian house occupied by the Inland Revenue. It was demolished in 1950 or 1951 to free the site for the forthcoming bus station. A late Victorian house at No. 2 is just visible beyond the Georgian building. This housed the offices of various Canterbury firms including W.E. Pinnock, removal and haulage contractors, and Frank Cooper, builders merchants.

After a long gap, including the site of the Congregational Church, is the white rendered end wall of the first of a row of two and three storey cottages at Nos. 9 to 15 Watling Street.
See CBB, Page 39 – Top
(Courtesy Canterbury Museums)

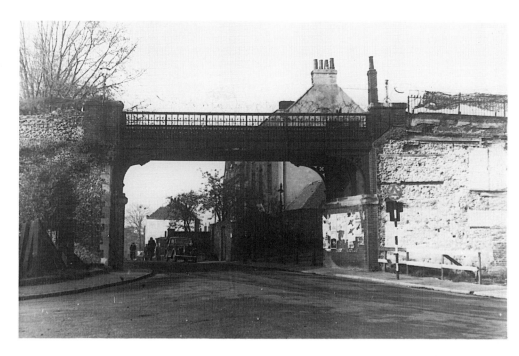

Up until the early 1930s, the Dane John Brewery stood on a large corner site between Watling Street and Marlowe Avenue. When the buildings were demolished, the City Council conceived the idea of building a Civic Centre on the site. The idea of a Civic Way, to link the Civic Centre with the Cathedral, was also mooted at this time. The whole concept was revived after the Blitz and included in the Holden Plan of 1945.

This late 1940s picture was taken from the old brewery site and looks across Marlowe Avenue to the premises of Premier Motor Policies Ltd at No. 2. On the Holden Plan, Marlowe Avenue was to be replaced by an elongated open space, situated alongside the Civic Centre. All the old buildings on the street's west side, including the one in the photograph, were to be demolished. The replacement Wilson Plan retained Marlowe Avenue, but designated the entire west side for government offices, necessitating the same amount of demolition.

(Fisk-Moore)

This fascinating picture dates from 1946 and was taken at the same time as the one at the top of the page. This time, the photographer has moved further down Watling Street. In the foreground is the cellar of No. 29 and the empty site of No. 30 Watling Street, both buildings being blitz victims. Further along on the same side of the street there was another gap, where Nos. 32 and 33 had been similarly destroyed. On the opposite side of the street can be seen the houses at Nos. 16 to 19 Watling Street, a wonderful group of Jacobean style buildings, dating from 1625. The gabled houses on the left (Nos. 18 & 19), had been gutted in 1942, but were considered important enough not to be demolished.

The Holden Plan treated this section of Watling Street with reverence. It intended to redevelop only those empty sites caused by the blitz and even the gutted Jacobean houses were to be retained. The Wilson Plan was almost the same, except that the gutted houses were to go. They were demolished in 1953.
See CBB, Page 18 and CAB, Page 13 – Middle
(Courtesy Canterbury Museums)

BUTCHERY LANE AND THE LONGMARKET

The blitz damaged Regency Corn Exchange and Longmarket building was demolished down to first floor level in mid June 1942. In the autumn of that year it was suggested that temporary shops for blitzed traders could be erected within the retained ground floor walls of the old Longmarket structure. However, these did not appear for another five years.

The 1945 Holden Plan revived an old pre-war planning concept from the early 1930s. This was for the construction of the Civic Way, a grand processional roadway to run from the Dane John (where civic offices were to be built), to Burgate Street and the Cathedral. The Civic Way idea was resurrected after the June 1942 blitz, incorporated into the Holden Plan, then scrapped along with the rest of the plan after the November 1945 elections (see also page 48).

The 1947 Wilson Road Plan included a scaled down version of the Civic Way that still crossed part of the Longmarket site. The rest of the area right up to Butchery Lane was destined to be an open market square.

In the meantime, the temporary shops idea was finally put in motion. The old picture was taken on 4th May 1947 and shows the first of the 'Ministry Huts' being erected on the Longmarket site. To the right of the concrete framework can be seen the surviving rear Gateway to the lost Corn Exchange–Longmarket building.

Behind the emerging prefabricated shops is a group of buildings situated on the north-east corner of Butchery Lane with Burgate Street. These were destined to be demolished to make way for the above mentioned open market square. But for now, with the chronic shortage of shop space, they were being retained.

See CAB, Page 58 and TAN, Page 9   (Bob Williams)

The above photograph was taken from a position just behind the old Barclays Bank premises (see page 26). The current picture was taken from exactly the same spot, now a loading bay just off Iron Bar Lane. In the foreground can be seen the rears of shops built in 1958 and fronting the Longmarket. The dummy chimneys and chimney pots of the new 'pastiche' Longmarket development are visible in the middle distance. This replaced the 'shoebox' Longmarket development which lasted from 1960 to 1990. This, in turn, replaced the 'pre-fab' Longmarket, being constructed in the old view above.

(Paul Crampton)

Another view from May 1947, showing the construction of the prefabricated shops on the Longmarket site. Beyond the newly erected concrete supports can be seen some of the surviving buildings situated on the east side of Butchery Lane. The brick building in the centre of the picture had clearly been fire damaged in the 1942 blitz. In fact, it is two shops: F.W. Finnis, the baker, (No. 13) and a currently empty shop at No. 14 Butchery Lane. The damaged timber frame on the end wall indicates that this building was quite an ancient structure with later brick elevations to the front and rear. The damaged upper storeys were dismantled in about 1949, leaving just the ground floor retail areas of both shops. To the right was a fairly modern shop at No. 15, being the premises of Court & Cooke Ltd, electrical engineers. Next came No. 16, which encompassed two old jettied timber framed buildings and was part of Court Bros Ltd. Finally, on the Burgate Street corner and visible in the picture opposite, a much larger building that was also part of Courts.

(Rob Williams)

A wonderful photograph of the now completed Longmarket prefabricated shops, taken from St George's Street in 1949. To the right is a surviving part of the front elevation of the lost Corn Exchange building. Part of a curved arch, originally leading into the ground floor Longmarket section, can clearly be made out. This stuccoed fragment was not the only trace of the old building to be found at this time. Further right still can just be seen a Doric column, also from the original façade and part of the entrance to J.H.G. Hamilton the wine merchants. They were still trading from premises that comprised largely surviving elements of the old Corn Exchange building, including a cellar. At the far end can be seen the rendered rear wall of the Burgate Street gateway, also from the old complex. Another interesting pre-war building is on the left, with the steep pitched roof and tall chimney. This is the bakehouse of F.W. Finnis and situated behind their Butchery Lane shop.
See CBB, Page 25 – Top, BOC, Page 14 – Middle and CAB, Back Cover

(Alan Stingemore)

The final picture dates from 1949 or 1950 and looks north along Butchery Lane from The Parade. Although the Midland Bank building dominates, what is of more interest are the various buildings along the east side of Butchery Lane, on the right. Nearest the camera is the premises of Burton Montague Ltd, a war damaged shop with the upper storeys removed. Next are four prefabricated shops, constructed at the same time as those on the adjacent Longmarket site. Finally are the aforementioned surviving shop buildings at Nos. 13 to 16 Butchery Lane. By this time, the fire damaged upper storeys of Nos. 13 and 14 had been dismantled.

The Holden Plan showed a tall narrow building, supported on round arches, to be built along the entire east side. This would have separated the lane from the new Civic Way and maintained its integrity as a lane. The replacement Wilson Plan opened up the east side completely to form part of an open market square.
See CBB, Page 59 – Top Right and TAN, Page 33 – Top left

(Fisk-Moore)

25

ST GEORGE'S STREET (NORTH WEST SECTION)

Barclays Bank at No. 23 St George's Street was one of a number of business premises to have survived the blitz, albeit in a truncated state. This bank building, new in the 1920s, was gutted in the 1st June 1942 raid, but unlike the shops on either side, something of it was salvaged. The fire damaged upper storeys of the main front portion of the building were dismantled and a new roof constructed over the surviving ground floor bank hall. The flat roofed single storey rear section of the bank premises had come through the blitz intact.

Other buildings to have survived in a truncated state included Slatters Hotel in St Margaret's Street and part of Beasleys in Stour Street.

The old photograph was taken in January 1949, when Barclays Bank had existed in this state for over six years. To the left of it and just out of the picture was the National Provincial Bank at No. 25 St George's Street. This had been very much more damaged in the blitz and had to be almost completely demolished. A new brick built single storey bank hall was then constructed on the old foundations.

Deep cellars that had once belonged to buildings lost in 1942 existed on both sides of Barclays Bank. On the left of the bank was Worlds Stores, grocers, (No. 24) and to the right, Dolcis shoe shop at No. 22. In late 1947 and early 1948 trenches were dug in these cellars to see if anything of archaeological significance could be found. As it turned out, the original sinking of these cellars had destroyed most medieval levels. Unfortunately, the surviving Roman levels yielded little of significance.

See CBB, Page 29 – Left and CAB, Pages 20 & 21 – Bottom Right

(Fisk-Moore)

The old Barclays Bank was finally dismantled in late 1953, just prior to the reconstruction of the present bank building on the same site. By this time a new shop building to its right was already completed and trading. Opened in November 1952, this new building included Dolcis Shoe Company (the new No. 13) and James Walker Jewellers (the new No. 11). The new Barclays Bank, now No. 9 St George's Street, was completed at the end of 1955. The National Provincial Bank also redeveloped on the old site. Their new premises (the new No. 7) opened in 1956.

(Paul Crampton)

This mid 1940s view shows the decimated western end of St George's Street and virtually intact Parade beyond. The only blitz casualty in The Parade was the former Rose Hotel, situated on the corner with Rose Lane. The still standing west wall, as well as a small part of the front elevation, can be seen on the left in the middle distance.

On the far right is the temporary National Provincial Bank mentioned on the opposite page. Beyond this is the surviving portion of the old Corn Exchange frontage, as described on page 25. At this time the prefabricated shops had not yet been put up.

Had the 1945 Holden Plan been implemented, then the Civic Way would have crossed at right angles to the main street, in the middle distance. Traffic along St George's Street would have become one-way, with traffic in the opposite direction being carried by the proposed parallel relief road.

See CBB, Page 24, TAN, Page 32 and CAB, Page 20.   (Messenger Group Newspapers)

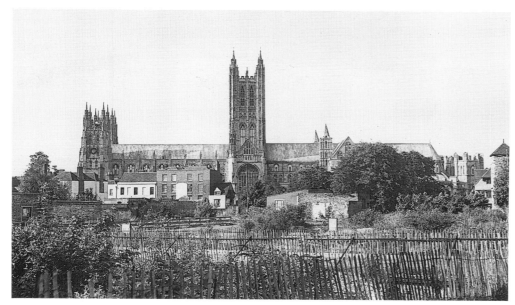

This is one of a number of panoramic views of the Cathdral, from across the blitzed wastelands, that are reproduced in this book. The photograph has been dated 1945, but is more likely to have been taken in the summer of 1947, because of the absence of the scaffolding on the south-west pinnacle of Bell Harry Tower. This had been removed in the winter of 1946 through to 1947. 1947 was the year that City Architect, Hugh L. Wilson, came up with the development plan for Canterbury that would be implemented in the 1950s. The main reason for the rejection of the 1945 Holden Plan was the 75 acres of compulsory purchase required, just to carry out the first stage of it. Wilson's plan required only 34 acres, concentrated almost entirely on the blitzed area of the city. When the accompanying picture was taken, the empty void on the north side of St George's Street was still a patchwork of privately owned sites of varying size.

On the left of the photograph can just be seen the flat-roofed rear extension of Barclays Bank, as mentioned opposite.

See CAB, Front Cover   (© RCHM)

A superb photograph of Canterbury's main thoroughfare, taken in the opposite direction to the one at the top of the page. Here, the intact buildings on either side of The Parade are in the foreground. The marching parade, consisting of naval personnel both past and present, is entering the St George's Street section of the main street with its few surviving buildings and vast empty spaces. Both the temporary banks can be seen on the north (left) side of the street, as can the gutted shell of St George's Church further up (see pages 36 and 37).

The twisting route of St George's Street (as well as its narrowness) is quite apparent from this angle. Both Holden and Wilson plans intended to straighten out the street, which meant that when the time came, the banks would be reconstructed further back on the new alignment. However, in the Wilson Plan, St George's Street was also to be made much wider as it was to take two-way traffic, as opposed to the one-way under Holden.

See CBB, Page 28 and CAB, Pages 24 and 25   (Bill Entwistle)

In 1952 the cellars seen in the old photograph were filled in and the site used to increase Rose Lane to its present width. That is why the current view is on Rose Lane and the old view just off. In 1953 the rest of the former Parade Chambers site, together with that of the Canterbury Club, were used to build a new shop for Barretts of Canterbury Ltd. This building, now occupied by C & H Fabrics, can just be seen on the right of the current picture. In the mid 1950s the former Rose Hotel site was also developed. This 'new' shop can be seen on the left.

(Paul Crampton)

ROSE LANE AND ST GEORGE'S STREET
(SOUTH-WEST SECTION)

In the summer of 1946, flushed with success at discovering the famous Roman mosaics, the Canterbury Excavation Committee moved their volunteer diggers into open cellars along Rose Lane. Their purpose was to establish if the Roman building (of which the mosaics formed part) found on the corner of Butchery Lane and the north side of The Parade, extended to the south side of the main street. The cellars in question consisted of two on the west side of Rose Lane that once belonged to the former Rose Hotel, lately the Rose Club. Three more were excavated on the east side of the same lane. Of these, two were once beneath the blitzed Parade Chambers (the former Bakers Hotel), and one below the Canterbury Club.

The accompanying photograph shows excavation in progress in one of the cellars relating to the Parade Chambers, designated cellar 'J' by the Canterbury Excavation Committee. Fascinated passers-by are crowding the chestnut paling fences along the Rose Lane and St George's Street frontages, hoping for the first glimpse of another exciting new Roman discovery. Sadly, they were to be disappointed. The cellars in question had been dug so deeply when they were created that most archaeological levels had been eliminated. However, enough evidence was gleaned to establish that the Roman building discovered earlier that spring did not extend into this area. As a consolation, a stone and tile lined Roman drain was found close to the main street on either side of the Rose Lane junction. This was particularly well preserved on the east side of Rose Lane (the side in the picture), as it ran through an area beneath the Parade Chambers, where no cellar had been dug, i.e. beneath the 16th century timber framed section of the lost building.

See CAB, Page 14 (Courtesy Canterbury Archaeological Trust)

This picture dates from 1947 and shows the large bomb site on the south side of St George's Street between Rose Lane (left) and the surviving Marks and Spencer shop (just out of sight on the right). This area was once occupied by the Canterbury Club (No. 33 St George's Street) to the right side of the site and The Parade Chambers (No. 31) on the left. Two round arches relating to the front cellar wall of the lost Canterbury Club building can be seen at the far end of the site against the St George's Street frontage. This cellar, designated 'Cellar L' by the Canterbury Excavation Committee, was included in the dig referred to on the opposite page. Evidence of pre-Roman occupation was found here in the form of a ditch and fragments of pottery.

The Civic Way, an integral part of the first stage Holden Plan, was destined to take up this entire area. On the Wilson Plan, the widened Rose Lane was to take up only the former site of The Parade Chambers. A new shop building was destined for the Canterbury Club site, which later turned out to be for Barretts.

(Rob Williams)

This interesting photograph was taken from St George's Street and has captured part of the south side of the street. The Rose Lane junction and the empty site seen in the picture on the left are hidden behind the ice cream van. The premises of Marks and Spencer Ltd, at Nos. 34 to 36 St George's Street, dominate this view. This firm, who always built from new at the time, put up this impressive shop building in 1930. The frontage was clearly inspired by the neo-classical design of the old Regency Corn Exchange building that once stood almost opposite. The Marks and Spencer shop received a large rear extension in 1939, on a site known as Rose Square, where some slum cottages had been demolished earlier that decade.

As is widely known, this was the only shop in St George's Street to have survived the 1942 blitz intact. Holden's Civic Way was destined to pass along the western (far) side of their shop. This would have given Marks and Spencer a commanding position in the new Canterbury.
See BOC, Page 14 – Top and CAB, Page 23 – Top) (Alan Stingemore)

Apart from Marks and Spencer, very little else could be found along the south street frontage, save a number of empty cellars. One such cellar is pictured here, being that once belonging to E. Bing & Son the chemists at No. 41 St George's Street. The ubiquitous Buddleia crowds in from both sides and has even seeded itself on the floor of this open cellar. The former site of E. Bing & Son also forms part of the dramatic old photograph reproduced on the back cover of this volume.

Although only cellars could be found on the street frontage, there were other surviving buildings set well back. These were concentrated only in the south-west section of St George's Street (i.e. between Marks and Spencer and Whitefriars Passage). Just to the east of Marks and Spencer was the single storey printing works of the Kentish Gazette (No. 39). Wooden sheds had been erected to augment the premises and replace their blitzed office building. Also set back from the street were some surviving buildings from the Simon Langton Girls School.
See CAB, Page 23 – Bottom (Mr A. Moody)

ST GEORGE'S STREET (NORTH-EAST SECTION)

One of the most remarkable archaeological discoveries in late 1940s Canterbury was the well preserved remains of a Roman Bath House on the north side of St George's Street in 1947. It was uncovered in four cellars along the street frontage, beneath where W.H. Smiths and Woolworths stand today.

Later in 1949, with time running out and reconstruction of the blitzed area imminent, the archaeologists hired a crane with a mechanical shovel and cleared a large area to the north of the St George's Street cellars. This was to find and record as much of ancient Canterbury as possible, before it was too late. Up until this time, the vast majority of investigations had taken place in large cellars adjacent to the main streets, with the Roman levels (if they still existed) just below the cellar floor. The area in question was too large to clear by hand, bearing in mind that only one small cellar had been sunk here.

The accompanying photograph shows the crane from local firm, Robert Brett, beginning this process. In the background can be seen St Thomas' Catholic Church and the old church tower of St Mary Magdalene, two lucky survivors of the blitz.

Of the discoveries made here, the most important was the 'T' junction of two Roman roads that helped to resolve the Roman street plan. In the centre of the area, roughly where the crane is standing, a small 16th century cellar was recorded.

The rebuilding of this area began in the autumn of 1951 when the construction of the new Woolworth store got underway. It opened for business in July of the following year.

See CBB, Page 28 and CAB, Pages 24 & 25)

(Courtesy Canterbury Archaeological Trust)

The new building next to Woolworths was completed in the spring of 1954. This included the new premises for W.H. Smith & Son Ltd, opened in May of that year. The summer of 1954 saw completion of the David Greig shop on the other side of Woolworths. The current photograph shows the new rear extension for Smiths, just completed. The design of the service lift tower has been influenced by the old church tower of St Mary Magdalene. This new contextual building extension is my own personal favourite of all the recent construction in Canterbury.

(Paul Crampton)

Few customers in the pre-war W.H. Smith shop could have realised that in the cellar beneath them existed substantial and visible remains of a large Roman building. This fact was discovered in 1947, when archaeological investigations were carried out in the open cellar of the former No. 17 St George's Street. Whilst cutting an exploratory trench, someone noticed that the lower part of the cellar's east wall was made from in-situ Roman material. The cellar is pictured here, with the Roman wall visible to the right of the scale marker.

In the 18th century the cellar diggers must have encountered this massive Roman wall and rather than attempt to remove it, decided to re-use its outer face as the inner face for the cellar. The cellar steps were then cut in behind the wall and can be seen in the centre of the picture. The ancient wall was identified as the west exterior wall of a Roman bath house, of which much more was discovered in adjacent cellars to the east.

See CBB, Page 29 – Top Right and CAB, Pages 24 & 25

(Courtesy Canterbury Archaeological Trust)

Another photograph of the clearance operation, prior to the massive archaeological investigation in the summer of 1949. I like this photograph, particularly because of the amount of tall vegetation surrounding the mechanical excavator. This area was covered with buildings before the June 1942 blitz; now it was a wilderness. However, the huge clump of Buddleia on the left and the seven year old tree saplings on the right would soon be devoured by the jaws of the crane. The cleared site would then be designated 'Area R' by the Canterbury Excavation Committee.

In the background to the left can be seen the shell of St George's Church and part of Loyns Bakery, both on the north side of St George's Street and beyond the junction for Canterbury Lane. It is interesting to note that the Bretts crane is working from a location that would now be smack in the middle of Woolworths.

(Courtesy Canterbury Archaeological Trust)

This picture dates from 1949 and is another wonderful view of the Cathedral, seen from across the empty void that is late 1940s St George's Street. This photograph was taken just to the east of Whitefriars Passage on the south side of the street, but offers a clear view of the north-east section of St George's Street, between Iron Bar Lane and Canterbury Lane. There is much less vegetation in evidence than in the 1947 view reproduced on page 27. This is largely because of the amount of archaeological investigation that had been carried out in the intervening years. This was a remarkable achievement by the Canterbury Excavation Committee and their band of amateur archaeologists, especially considering that digs were carried out in holiday periods only.

All the archaeological information described in this book has been obtained from 'The Archaeology of Canterbury', volume VII, subtitled 'Excavations in the St George's Street and Burgate Street areas', published by the Canterbury Archaeological Trust and available from them.

See CBB, Front Cover

(Courtesy Canterbury Archaeological Trust)

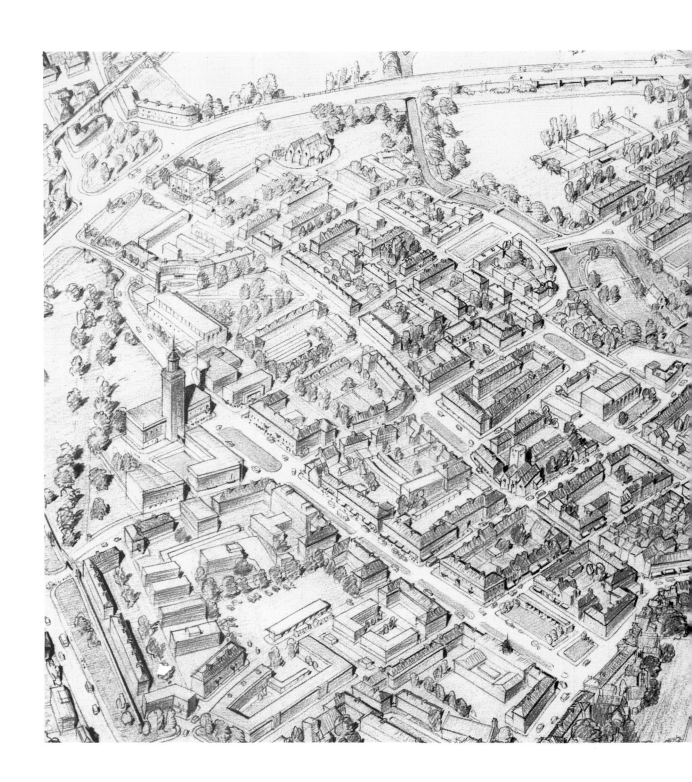

IMAGINATIVE BIRDSEYE VIEW C

COMPLETED HOLDEN PLAN

(Courtesy Canterbury Museums)

ST GEORGE'S STREET (SOUTH-EAST SECTION)

It is hard to believe that such a rural scene was captured in the main street of Canterbury. The photograph dates from 1948 and features the Buffs Regiment parading along St George's Street, on the occasion of their freedom of the city ceremony. The backdrop is the empty cellars and bomb sites along the south side of the street. This huge void stretched from the old Kentish Gazette premises (just visible in the background of the old view) next to Marks and Spencer, right up to the city wall and cattle market near to St George's crossroads.

The empty site on the left was once occupied by Marlowe House, the premises of Jays Furnishing Stores at Nos. 57 and 58 St George's Street. The painted sign amidst the Buddleia confirms this fact. Historically, No. 57 was also reputed to be the birthplace of Christopher Marlowe.

Next is the narrow St George's Lane, heading off to the left, with chestnut paling fences to mark its position. On the other side of the lane junction is the former site of the Coach and Horses public house, of which nothing remains save the pub cellar. Again, a white painted sign tells passers-by what stood here before the blitz.

Further along on the same side of the street, in 1949, a large Roman apsed building was discovered in cellars that were situated opposite St George's Church. This middle section of the south side of St George's Street appears to be covered in dense foliage. Trees can be seen, but these are too mature to have grown on the bomb sites. In fact, they are standing in the small garden areas, once hidden behind the now lost shops and houses.

See CBB, Page 33 – Top Left and CAB, Page 27 – Top   (Fisk-Moore)

The decision, in 1951, to retain the tower of St George's Church meant that the planned widened St George's Street had to be slewed over to the south. This new trajectory, as well as the vastly widened junction for St George's Lane, swallowed up most of the old sites mentioned above. The filled-in cellars of Jays and the Coach and Horses are, therefore, now under the main street. The new shops either side of the now broadened St George's Lane were built in the late 1950s and early 1960s. St George's Street was pedestrianised in the early 1970s.

(Paul Crampton)

It is hard to believe that this 1947 picture was taken from a location now occupied by the bus station and modern shops. The photographer is standing on the vast bomb site between St George's Lane (left), the south side of St George's Street and St George's Terrace (out of sight to the right). This view was taken well back from the cellars on the St George's Street frontage that can be seen on the opposite page.

The wild flowers in the foreground are growing in the former back gardens of the lost houses fronting St George's Terrace. In 1949 a number of exploratory archaeological trenches were cut across this area. A collection of 4th century Roman coins was found, as well as traces of the Roman bank that would have existed against the inside of the city wall.

The ruins of St George's Church are visible in this picture, as they are in a number of other views reproduced on these pages.
See CAB, Page 34 (Rob Williams)

Another view of the gothic window, but showing the entire east facing wall between the two turns in the north wall. With so much post-medieval repair work, there is a chance that this architectural feature was not in-situ before the dissolution.

(Courtesy Canterbury Local Study Centre)

The blitz wiped out all the buildings on the south side of St George's Street, between Whitefriars Passage and St George's Lane. This exposed not only the trees in the small back garden areas, but also a long ancient wall beyond the vegetation. This wall, running parallel to St George's Street, once related to the north wall of Whitefriars Church and contained remains of it. At one point the wall made a 90 degree turn southwards for a short stretch, before making another 90 degree turn to resume its original course. Within this short length of east facing wall was a blocked gothic style window. This can be seen in the accompanying photograph. At first it appears to be a doorway, but the plinth (the projecting base of the wall) is unbroken. As was the case with the long north facing wall, the pictured section contained large amounts of post-medieval brickwork and re-used medieval demolition material. This probably occurred when some of the ruinous church walls were repaired and became the perimeter wall for the post dissolution manor house and, later, the Simon Langton Schools.

(Courtesy Canterbury Local Study Centre)

This photograph looks across the site of lost buildings on the south side of St George's Street, including that of the Kentish Observer at No. 49. Behind the vegetation can be seen part of the aforementioned Whitefriars north wall.

See CAB, Page 26 (Mr A. Moody)

ST GEORGE'S CHURCH

This photograph offers a view of St George's Church rarely seen. Most pictures of the gutted shell of the church were taken from St George's Street. However, this view, taken by Alan Stingemore, is from the north-east, at a location just off Burgate Lane. Much of what can be seen from this angle dates from the Victorian expansion of 1872. The gabled wall on the left belongs to the 19th century chancel and behind it the altar was situated. To its right is the east end gabled wall of the north aisle, also Victorian work. The north wall of the church can also just be seen behind the overgrown churchyard shrubs. A considerable amount of glass in the windows along the north wall had survived the June 1942 fire, although little was left intact by the end of the decade, when this picture was taken.

The entire shell of St George's Church and its churchyard was to be retained intact on the Holden Plan of 1945, to become a permanent memorial to the blitz of Canterbury. When this plan was voted out in

the autumn election of the same year, the future of the church became a lot less certain. Ironically, the Canterbury Citizens Defence Association, who successfully put up candidates against the Holden Plan in the 1945 autumn election, were not in favour of retaining the ruins of St George's Church. The anti-compulsory purchase–pro private development shop owners' lobby in the CCDA far outnumbered the conservationists with whom they had allied themselves.

The new alignment of St George's Street could not be decided upon until the fate of the church was known. Its complete demolition would have allowed for the straightening of the main street and the provision of more retail space.

By the end of the 1940s the complete shell still stood and nothing had yet been decided for certain.

See CAB, Page 37 – Top and TAN, Page 47 – Top (Alan Stingemore)

By the early 1950s the fate of the church ruin had been decided and a compromise was reached. The tower alone was to be retained because of its 12th century elements. In October 1952 the standing walls of the rest of the church were demolished. The church tower was restored in 1953 and 1954. Then in 1955 a terrace of shops was built around the now lone church tower. These shops were pulled down in late 1990. The following year saw a fascinating archaeological investigation of the former church site. The new shops seen in the current photograph were completed in 1993.

(Paul Crampton)

A wonderful photograph of the tower and ruinous south wall of St George's Church. The photographer is standing at the St George's Lane junction and looking westwards along St George's Street. It is clear from this picture just how narrow the street was near the church tower. Two double deck buses could only pass each other here with difficulty.

As is mentioned opposite, the Holden Plan retained the entire shell of St George's Church. The potential bottleneck problem would have been eased by the fact that, under Holden, the existing main street would carry only one-way traffic. The new parallel cross city relief road would take traffic in the opposite direction. The quickly aborted interim plan of 1946, formulated by the new CCDA-backed council, did away with the church ruins entirely, preferring to redevelop the site for retail purposes.

See CBB, Page 30 and CAB, Page 28 (Messenger Group Newspapers)

This picture is a close up of the south face of the tower, as it appeared throughout the late 1940s. The scaffolding and bracing were put round the tower during July 1942, following the failed attempt to pull the church down. The belfry window was bricked up at the same time, to strengthen the top of the tower. This had been severely weakened by the demolition attempt.

The original subject of the photograph was the tower clock, judging by its position in the picture. This clock, familiar to many generations of Canterbury citizens, was a late 19th century addition to the street scene. Before the blitz the tower contained five bells, ranging in diameter from 28 to 40 inches. A 'modern' chiming apparatus had been fitted between the wars, as the bells could no longer be rung by hand. This was because of the unsure state of the timber framework within the belfry. Presumably all the bells had thundered to the ground and were destroyed when the tower was gutted on 1st June 1942.

(Bill Entwistle)

The gutted shell of the church appears here as it was often pictured in the late 1940s, as opposed to the much rarer view reproduced on the opposite page. St George's Lane and its junction into St George's Street can be seen in the foreground. The photograph dates from 1946, a time when the remains of St George's Church seemed doomed. It is unclear if the Wilson Plan, as conceived in 1947, intended to retain the tower or remove the church ruin in its entirety. Contemporary plans are unclear, but I have included it in the map, reproduced on page 17.

The Canterbury Archaeological Society and the Ancient Monuments Board both wanted at least the tower to be retained. However, councillor J.G.B. Stone declared at the time that it should be pulled down. The controversy over the 'Tumbledown Tower' was even reported in the Evening News on 3rd March 1950 as holding up the £1,000,000 redevelopment of Canterbury.

See CAB, Page 31 – Top (Fisk-Moore)

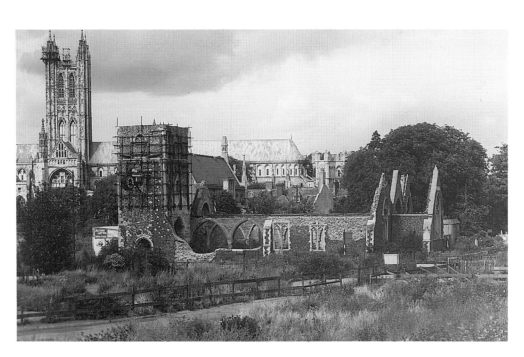

GRAVEL WALK

Gravel Walk was once longer but much narrower than it is today. It left Rose Lane at a junction opposite St Mary Bredin church and followed roughly along the route it does today. Then, just after St George's Lane joined it from the left, Gravel Walk climbed steeply to meet St George's Terrace atop the city wall ramparts.

War damage was not too serious and well over 50% of Gravel Walk's buildings lasted until the 1960s. The old photograph was taken in 1947 and shows the derelict vehicles of Philpots garage that had been left resting and rusting for five years.

The premises of E.J. Philpot Ltd could be found on the south side of Gravel Walk. The white rendered wall behind belongs to the private residence at No. 3 Gravel Walk. Beyond the house, on the same side of the street, could be found another garage later used by Drews Coaches. Then came the remote burial ground of St Mary Bredin Church, followed by part of the premises of W.S. William & Son – coach builders. Finally, there was a large private residence on the corner with Rose Lane.

On the opposte side of Gravel Walk and just visible in the top right corner of the old picture were the science buildings belonging to Simon Langton Boys School. These stretched along a third of the length of the north side. On the same side, and nearer the Rose Lane end, could be found a length of ancient flint wall, much of which used to form the perimeter wall of the Augustinian Whitefriars.

(Rob Williams)

The north side of Gravel Walk was cleared in the summer of 1960, after the Simon Langton Boys School had relocated. Then, in 1963, Gravel Walk and St George's Lane were widened to their present width. The south side, including the old Philpots site, finally disappeared in 1965, to make way for a large surface car park. In 1969 St George's Lane was extended through to Watling Street and crossed part of the site of Philpots Garage. The multi-storey car park was built in the same year. Its stair-well, seen in the current picture, is also on the old garage site.

(Paul Crampton)

This late 1940s photograph is the only one I have ever seen of the sloping section of Gravel Walk that existed between St George's Terrace and the junction with St George's Lane. The wooden barrier was erected in 1942, to protect pedestrians from the long drop, resulting from the demolition of the gutted houses fronting St George's Terrace. The triple gabled building, prominent in the picture, stands on the west side of St George's Lane below. It is the 'new' extension to Simon Langton Boys School, constructed in 1914. Within this block could be found classrooms 15, 16 and 17 on the first floor, with the gymnasium below.

The Holden Plan of 1945 kept Gravel Walk as a narrow lane on its existing route, including the slope from St George's Terrace. However, new buildings were to be constructed at intervals along both sides. The Wilson Plan did away with the slope and routed the cross city relief road along Gravel Walk. An extended St George's Lane would act as a feeder onto the new relief road. Both narrow byways would be widened considerably as a result.

(Courtesy Ted Yeoman)

Another fascinating picture of the derelict Gravel Walk garage, as seen in 1947. As well as the remains of the three old cars, the rusting chassis and cab of an ancient lorry can be seen in this view. The photographer and contributor Rob Williams, who once attended the Simon Langton Boys School opposite, well remembers the old garage in happier days. In the early 1930s it was known as the Langton Garage, run by Mr G. Deakin and Mr R. Pollard. The garage used to provide a charabanc to take the junior boys to the school sportsfield at Nackington, well outside Canterbury. It was to this site that the school relocated in late 1959. The old school buildings, situated between the north side of Gravel Walk and St George's Street, were demolished the following year. The mid 1960s clearance of the south side of Gravel Walk included two former garage premises, two large detached houses and the St Mary Bredin burial ground (see below).

(Rob Williams)

This haven of peace and tranquillity could be found half way along Gravel Walk on the south side. It is the remote burial ground for St Mary Bredin Church that stood in nearby Rose Lane until its demolition in 1942. The burial ground was created shortly after the 1868 extension to the church had been built on the then existing graveyard. The 1874 ordnance survey map shows the Gravel Walk plot as a garden, but it must have assumed its later role at about that time.

The Holden Plan retained the burial ground exactly as it was. The replacement Wilson Plan of 1947 designated this area as a public open space. Presumably this would have meant moving the gravestones to the edges of the area and the provision of seating, as has happened elsewhere in Canterbury. However, its ultimate fate was to be very different. In about 1966 the gravestones and trees were removed entirely and the site tarmacked over to form part of a large car park. The old burial ground is now itself buried beneath the multi-storey car park.
See TAN, Page 5 – Bottom

(Messenger Group Newspapers)

ST GEORGE'S GATE

The accompanying picture (also to be seen on the front cover) was taken in the autumn of 1949 and shows St George's Gate, a street name that no longer exists. The 'temporary' premises of E.R. Bates, the gun shop, has attracted the attention of the only passers-by in the vicinity. It is situated on the site of their former premises, blitzed and then demolished in 1942.

The tall wall seen behind the Bates premises is actually a fragment of the medieval city wall, although bricks from the blitzed shop still adhere to it. The photographer from the Fisk-Moore studio has also captured the site of the former Fisk-Moore retail shop, which once stood between the Bates shop and the junction with Burgate Lane.

In the background can be seen the east end of the burnt out St George's Church and the chimney of Loyns Bakery in Canterbury Lane. The trees are standing in St George's Churchyard. Further back still, the Catholic church of St Thomas conceals the nave, but not the towers of Canterbury Cathedral, a magnificent sight from any angle.

The 1945 Holden Plan contained a novel idea for St George's Gate. It showed a large rectangular 'roundabout' for the proposed ring road sited across most of the area seen in the old photograph. In the centre of it, in a hollowed out area, were to have been the exposed drum tower bases of the old St George's City Gate. The later Wilson Plan scrapped this idea and showed a more conventional roundabout, sited slightly further to the east.

See CBB, Page 34, BOC, Page 14 – Bottom and CAB, Page 36

(Fisk-Moore)

St George's Gate was a short stretch of the main street, created in 1801, following the demolition of the above mentioned St George's City Gate. It was taken down to early 19th century ground level, but much of it still remains below ground within the buried city ditch. The fragment of medieval city wall was demolished in 1963, at a time when relics such as this were considered unimportant. The street itself finally ceased to be in 1969, when St George's Roundabout was constructed. The Bates shop disappeared for good at the same time.

(Paul Crampton)

Another superb picture of St George's Gate, taken by Fisk-Moore in 1949. The photographer has moved further back onto St George's Crossroads, to capture a wider area. On the right can be seen the edge of Pettit & Son, tobacconists, at No. 1 St George's Gate. This was the only building in this short stretch of the main street to have survived the blitz and its aftermath. There is also a much clearer view of the east end of St George's Church.

Although many post-medieval buildings would have had to be demolished to implement the Holden Plan, there was great care taken to protect important medieval structures. St George's Church ruin, of which about 60 per cent was medieval, was to be retained. Furthermore, the proposed St George's Roundabout was carefully positioned to expose the surviving drum tower bases of St George's City Gate. This is probably to the credit of Mr H.M. Enderby, the City Engineer and co-author of the plan. He loved Canterbury and was very knowledgeable about its history and ancient buildings.

See CAB, Page 37 – Bottom   (Fisk-Moore)

This book contains a number of pictures of a religious procession through Canterbury. It was part of a Catholic pilgrimage from Jerusalem that occurred in either 1949 or 1950. The photographs are very useful for their backdrops of the city before the redevelopment, especially as such views are so rare.

The one reproduced here shows the procession passing from St George's Gate to Lower Bridge Street. On the left can be seen the aforementioned tobacconists' shop of Pettit & Son. To the right is part of the much larger Co-op premises at Nos. 11 and 12 Lower Bridge Street. This shop had been damaged in the blitz, but was now fully repaired and trading.

Although Holden's elongated roundabout was a different shape and in a slightly different position to the one later proposed by Wilson, both versions necessitated the demolition of Pettits and the Co-op. The latter was removed in 1961, the former in 1969.

See TAN, Page 20   (Fisk-Moore)

The accompanying photograph shows St George's Crossroads in the late 1940s, with Upper Bridge Street in the foreground, St George's Gate to the left and Lower Bridge Street furthest from the camera. The picture includes many buildings that would need to be sacrificed to provide post-war Canterbury with a ring road. These include the aforementioned Pettits and Co-op buildings, both visible on the left. All of the post-war development plans, both unofficial and unofficial, included a complete ring road. In every case it was destined to pass through the area shown in the picture. Holden's ring road and St George's Roundabout were to be built in the plan's first development stage. This did not require the demolition of any of the buildings just seen to the right of the photograph. The Wilson version of St George's Roundabout was placed more centrally onto the crossroads. However, as first conceived, the roundabout was smaller than the one that was eventually built in 1969.

See TAN, Pages 20 and 21

(Messenger Group Newspapers)

VIEWS FROM ST GEORGE'S TERRACE

Relatively few photographs were taken of Canterbury in the late 1940s, unlike the periods immediately after the blitz, or during the reconstruction in the early 1950s, which are both well represented. This has been a particular problem for me, trying to cover this interim period. Of the photographs that were taken, a number were from the higher vantage point of St George's Terrace. This offered a panoramic view across the overgrown wastelands of the blitzed and levelled St George's Parish, as well as spectacular views of the Cathedral and the substantial remains of St George's Chuch.

In the accompanying mid-1940s picture, the Kent Messenger photographer has resisted the above-mentioned temptations. Rather, he has turned his camera to the right to capture the top end of St George's Street, the buildings on either side of Burgate Lane and the rear of the large Co-op premises at St George's Crossroads.

In the foreground can be seen St George's Terrace itself, with the familiar post-blitz chestnut paling fence, erected to protect passers-by from the sharp drop beyond. Clumps of Red Valerian have already established themselves on the old foundations. The late Georgian and Regency houses that once stood where the fence is now had basements at normal ground level and their main front entrances accessible from St George's Terrace, that runs on top of the old city wall rampart. In the late 1940s no trace of these houses could be seen from St George's Terrace. However, from St George's Lane the front cellar walls with their large round arches could be seen along the side of the earth bank beneath the city wall rampart.

See CBB, Page 36 and CAB, Page 39 – Middle

(Messenger Group Newspapers)

The suggested siting of the new bus station on the plot of land between here and St George's Lane was first mooted in the 1947 Wilson Plan. In 1955 the site in question was cleared for construction to begin. This work necessitated cutting into the earth bank beneath St George's Terrace. During this process a square Roman tower was discovered. This formed part of the Roman city wall, but faced inwards unlike the more familiar medieval bastions that project out into the city ditch. The Roman tower was bricked over in early 1956 as the building of the bus station went ahead.

(Paul Crampton)

This is the more usual view captured from St George's Terrace in the late 1940s. This 1949 photograph is very similar to the spectacular 1946 picture reproduced on page 1, except for the removal of the scaffolding from Bell Harry Tower. This panoramic view would have been lost, had the 1945 Holden Plan been implemented. The planners were clearly inspired by pre-war St George's Terrace and proposed two blocks of new houses be built along the terrace, one on either side of the central Gravel Walk slope. The existing slopes at either end were to be done away with and replaced by sloping feeder roads from St George's Lane, at roughly 90 degrees to St George's Terrace.

The 1947 Wilson Plan identified the area in the foreground to be the site of the new bus station. This would allow unobstructed views of the Cathedral to continue from an undeveloped St George's Terrace. Sadly, the gargantuan early 1960s Ricemans department store put paid to that idea.
See CBB, Page 32 and BOC, Page 32 – Middle
(Courtesy Canterbury Archaeological Trust)

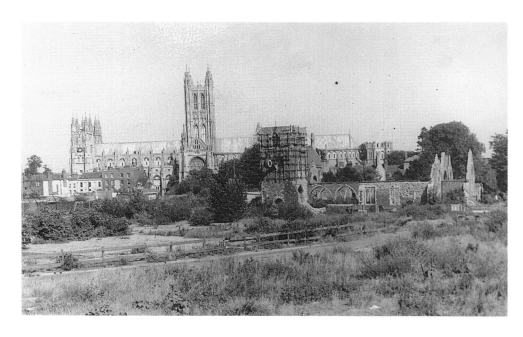

Another photograph of the Catholic religious procession coming into Canterbury. They are seen here proceeding up the slope from St George's Gate and onto St George's Terrace. Another picture taken by Fisk-Moore, but not reproduced here, shows that the pilgrims held a religious ceremony on St George's Terrace.

The two large trees in full summer foliage are standing on the south side of St George's Gate at the end of the cattle market. In the distance on the right can be seen the premises of G. Twyman & Son Ltd, situated at St George's Crossroads. The area of chestnut paling on the right fences off a collapsed section of the city wall, where a high explosive bomb had landed in 1942. As mentioned above, the St George's Terrace slopes from St George's Gate at the north end and Watling Street to the south were to be eliminated in the Holden Plan. The Wilson Plan kept the slopes, but wanted no new buildings for St George's Terrace.
See TAN, Page 11 – Top (Fisk-Moore)

A view from St George's Terrace in the opposite direction to the one at the top of the page showing the old cattle market, Upper Bridge Street and the row of Lime trees that separate them. This picture can be dated to late 1948, or 1949, by the film 'Johnny Belinda' advertised on the Regal Cinema hoarding on the far side of Upper Bridge Street. The large gap on that side of the street was a result of enemy action. Six properties at Nos. 4 to 9 were lost here in 1942. A surviving building at No. 3 Upper Bridge Street can just be seen on the left. In 1949 this was a dental surgery.

The small cattle sale or auction has drawn an equally small crowd. This is in sharp contrast to pre-war cattle auctions, the old pictures of which show scores of on-lookers from St George's Terrace and Upper Bridge Street, as well as many dozens more cattle.
See CBB, Page 39 – Middle (Alan Stingemore)

UPPER BRIDGE STREET AND THE CATTLE MARKET

For many decades the Canterbury cattle market was situated on a strip of land between the city wall and Upper Bridge Street. More anciently the site had been occupied by the city defensive ditch or moat, but had long since been filled in.

The old photograph was taken in about 1949 and shows the cattle market with its wooden pens assembled in readiness for another market day. This scene could well be mistaken for one captured before the blitz, were it not for the absence of the beautiful Georgian and Regency terraced houses of St George's Terrace atop the city wall.

The city wall along this stretch looks very different from the way it was before the cattle market was built and different again from the way it appears today. Sometime around the beginning of the last century the old city wall bastions had been removed and much of the city wall

re-faced with red brick. At about the same time most of the semi-circular auctioneers' chambers were cut into the wall fabric. Some of the original flint facing can still be seen in areas along the wall. The plant Red Valerian can be seen rooted in the chalk mortar in between the flints, very much as it does today in the city wall along Broad Street.

In the far distance, the buildings around St George's Crossroads can be seen and, in particular, the white rendered walls of the shop premises of G. Twyman & Son Ltd. The far end of the cattle market appears to be in use as a car park. This use was extended over the entire area in 1955, after a new purpose built cattle market was constructed along Market Way.

See CBB, Page 37 (Bill Entwistle)

In 1958 construction of a facsimile of the medieval city wall was begun along this stretch. The old auctioneers' chambers were sealed for good, but still exist beneath the new flint facing. Two of the three original bastions were rebuilt (Nos. 6 and 7 in the defensive circuit). Number 5, which once stood adjacent to the Riding Gate, was not rebuilt. This is because the modern Watling Street junction partly covers the old site. However, the original position of the mission bastion has been marked out in the road and footway.

(Paul Crampton)

The Riding Gate public house sustained damage in a minor raid during 1942. By the mid 1940s, when this picture was taken, the blitz damage had still not been repaired. The inn was not open for business but the undamaged part of it was in use for storage.

The site of some lost cottages, as well as the cattle market, can be seen in Upper Bridge Street to the right. Before the blitz other cottages also stood to the left of the inn, between it and the Riding Gate itself. The address of the Riding Gate public house was No. 7 Old Dover Road. At this time, Watling Street changed to Old Dover Road as it passed under the Riding Gate Bridge (see page 23).

Both the Holden and Wilson Plans did away with this building: Holden to create an open space in front of the city wall and Wilson to make room for a roundabout. In the meantime, the inn was repaired and re-opened. The 1949 Kelly Street Directory lists the Riding Gate inn, with Alfred Banham as publican.

See CBB, Page 38

(Messenger Group Newspapers)

This interesting picture shows a close up of one of the auctioneer's chambers, associated with the cattle market. A row of these can be seen in the picture opposite. They probably date from 1830, the same year as the nearby city pound was built. These chambers were cut through the surviving core of the city wall and into the earth bank behind. The wall and bank dated from both Roman and medieval periods. St George's Terrace is immediately above the auctioneers' chambers, running along the rampart on top of the old earth bank. The cellars of the lost houses of St George's Terrace were also cut into the earth bank.

By 1946, when this photograph was taken, the old chamber featured had become the premises of Auto Auctions of Canterbury. They held sales of cars, motor cycles and commercial vehicles in the cattle market every Wednesday at 11.45 a.m. On this particular Wednesday a veteran car was for sale, the proceeds from which were to go towards the construction of the Battle of Britain memorial, to be put up at Dover.

(Fisk-Moore)

The final picture has captured the north end of the cattle market near to St George's Crossroads. The collection of late 1940s street furniture and cattle market featured is interesting, particularly as they have all since disappeared from this site. In the centre of the photograph can be seen the old weighing mechanism. It was removed in the early 1950s and one hopes it was given a good home. Just to the right of it and further back a tall stone monument is visible. This is the memorial to all the men of the Royal East Kent Yeomanry. By 1954 it had been moved to the former site of St Mary Bredman Church in the High Street (see page 15). A utility bodied East Kent bus trundles along the St George's Gate section of the main street. Another of this type is visible in the main picture on page 28. As the years passed, more features disappeared from this scene. By 1970 only St George's Clocktower was left.

(Messenger Group Newspapers)

LOWER BRIDGE STREET

Much of Lower Bridge Street survived the 1942 blitz. One high explosive bomb destroyed the shops at Nos. 6 to 10, but the rest of the street could still be found in the late 1940s. The old photograph was taken right at the end of this period, probably in the latter half of 1949. It shows surviving buildings on both sides. On the left of the picture can be seen the intact properties of No. 4 down to No. 1 Lower Bridge Street. The greengrocers shop of J. Hoare at No. 5 had also survived the bombing, but was damaged. It was later dismantled, retaining only the ground floor retail section. Adjacent to this was built a new temporary single storey shop for Tice & Co. Engineers (No. 6), whose old premises had been completely destroyed. The single storey shops can be seen nearest the camera and behind the lorry.

The east side of Lower Bridge Street is just visible on the right of the photograph. Many of the old properties along this side belonged to Invicta Motors.

The aborted Holden Plan of 1945 and the subsequent Wilson Plan both showed Lower Bridge Street as part of the proposed ring road, the former as a wide single carriageway, the latter as a dual carriageway. However, in both cases, the new ring road necessitated the demolition of all the buildings on the west side (left of the picture). This may account for the temporary nature of the repairs to the buildings here. The exposed fire places could still be seen in 1969.

Hidden behind these properties was the city wall and Zoar Chapel. At this time many Canterbury citizens were unaware of their existence behind the Lower Bridge Street buildings.

See CAB, Page 41 – Bottom and TAN, Page 21 – Bottom

(Messenger Group Newspapers)

The current picture shows Zoar Chapel and the city wall that were exposed when the buildings were demolished in 1969 for the second stage of the ring road. The original idea was to complete the ring road circuit and expose the city wall along the entire length of Broad Street, right down to Northgate. This never came to pass, although it would have been splendid to see the complete city wall. However, the cancellation of the third stage of the ring road did save a lot of buildings. Invicta Motors rebuilt their Lower Bridge Street premises in the early 1960s.

(Paul Crampton)

One day in July 1949 disaster struck at Invicta Motors, whose premises extended along much of the east side of Lower Bridge Street. A lorry delivering petrol had just reversed into one of the main garage areas. Before climbing out of his cab, the driver lit up a cigarette. It was to be his last. The resultant explosion blew the driver's cab roof off and started a fire that quickly engulfed adjacent vehicles. The photographer from the Fisk-Moore Studio, then situated only 100 yards away in Burgate Street, was quickly on the scene. This dramatic photograph was one of the first he took and shows the firemen tackling the blaze around the unlucky petrol tanker. Its distorted cab is quite apparent in this close up shot. The fire also spread to the roof of the garage building, but was quickly brought under control. Fortunately, damage to the actual premises was limited, although a number of brand new cars were badly scorched.

(Courtesy Invicta Motors Ltd)

The ambulances and fire fighting equipment are gathered here as a result of the rather bizarre accident detailed above. The blitz surviving properties at Nos. 1 to 4 Lower Bridge Street provide an interesting backdrop to the emergency service vehicles of the period. There are actually five properties in this row and not four as the numbering would suggest. On the far right is the Star Brewery Stores of George Beer & Rigden Ltd (No. 1A). To its left, and visible between the two ambulances, is Crayford House at No. 1, a doctor and dentist's surgery. No. 2 Lower Bridge Street is where Mac Fisheries Ltd, fishmongers, could be found in 1949. The site of their blitzed shop building can be seen in the 1940s picture on the back page. In the early 1950s Mac Fisheries moved back to St George's Street and into newly built premises, close to the site of their original shop.

At No. 3 Lower Bridge Street is Lorna Hairdressers, where 'Wella Permanent Waving' could be obtained. Finally at No. 4 is Dyson, confectioner and restaurant.

(Courtesy Invicta Motors Ltd)

This photograph was taken in May 1950, during Invicta Motors' Canterbury Service Week. By this time they had recovered from the fire and their premises were fully operational once more. The veteran car was known as 'The Old Crock' and is being driven by Mr J.B. Thompson with Mr Raymond Mayers as passenger.

On the right of the picture and beyond Invicta's showrooms can be seen the three storey building standing on the corner with Church Street St Paul's. It is the only building existing in this period that can be found in Lower Bridge Street today. On the left is the side of the Saracens Head public house, situated on the corner with Burgate Street. Another picture of this large inn can be seen on page 57.

Both sides of Lower Bridge Street were included in the 75 acres compulsory purchase area on the first stage Holden Plan. However, no demolition on the street's east side was envisaged in this initial development stage.
See TAN, Pages 44 and 45

(Courtesy Invicta Motor Ltd)

This is an imaginative drawing of the Civic Way that formed a significant part of the 1945 Holden Plan. The artist, who is standing by the theoretical new Civic Centre, looks north along the Civic Way towards Burgate Street and the Cathedral at the far end. In the foreground, Watling Street crosses the Civic Way at right angles. It is interesting to note that the artist should have depicted the old Jacobean houses in Watling Street, on the left of his impression, as they were to be retained (see page 23). Instead, he has drawn a new block of buildings in their place. Further along the Civic Way the places where the relief road and main street cross it can just be made out.

(Courtesy Canterbury Museums)

Below: This late 1940s picture shows the route that the Civic Way would have taken had the Holden Plan been implemented. The photographer is standing further north than the artist's impression above. In fact, this is the site where Holden's cross-city relief road would have traversed the Civic Way. In the 1947 Wilson Plan the Civic Way was replaced by a widened Rose Lane. This was to be bisected at a staggered cross roads by Wilson's more southerly version of the parallel relief road. Effectively, the widened Rose Lane was another Civic Way in all but name. This road was completed in 1965, but the Civic Centre it was planned to serve was never built.
See CAB, Page 15 – Bottom

(Courtesy Canterbury Archaeological Trust)

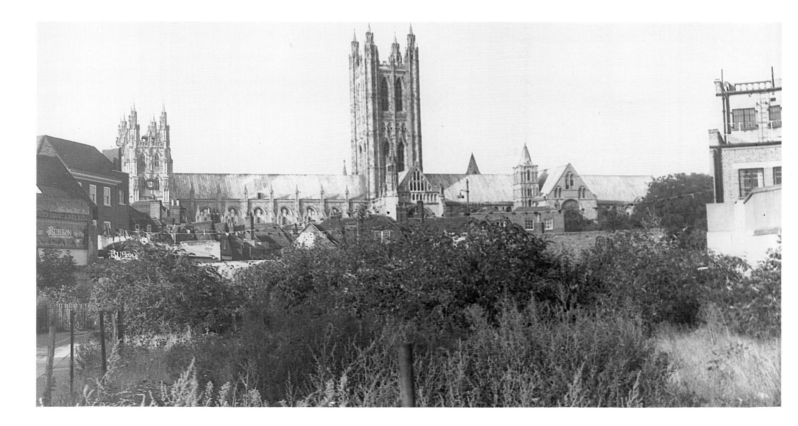

The Town Clerk, Mr John Boyle, on the far left, discusses the Holden Plan with some of his colleagues. They are, from left to right: Alderman Barrett, an elected member of the council, Mr H.M. Enderby, the City Engineer, and nearest the camera Mr L. Hugh Wilson, City Architect and the man responsible for the plan that replaced Holden's. The group are standing round a three dimensional model of the first stage development of the Holden Plan. This beautifully detailed model was constructed by Mr H. Olle and used in the spring of 1945, when the plan was unveiled to the public. The 3-D model was almost identical to the first stage development plan on paper, reproduced on page 16. However, the model did not include the open squares along Hawks Lane or at Orange Street.

(Fisk-Moore)

Below: This plan takes a small section of Canterbury and shows what would have happened had the Holden Plan been completed. When the Holden Plan is referred to in this book, it is always the 1945 first stage of the development that is discussed. This is because it was the first stage that was presented to the public and, in fact, rejected by them. The completed Holden Plan affected almost the entire city. It would have been so destructive that it is hard to imagine its completion being allowed, even if the first stage had been implemented. A more general map of the completed Holden Plan for all of Canterbury can be seen on page 64 and in an artists birds eye view at the centre of this book.

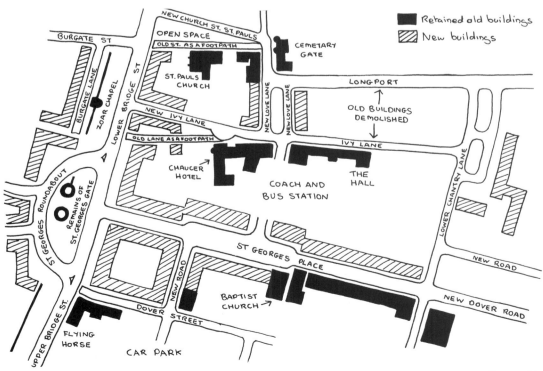

PAUL CRAMPTON. NOV 93

ST GEORGE'S PLACE (SOUTH SIDE)

This fascinating photograph of St George's Place was taken towards the end of the 1940s by veteran Canterbury photographer, Mr W. Fisk-Moore. He is standing in the Buddleia covered cellar of his blitzed photographic studio, at No. 7 St George's Place. The front cellar walls, seen against the north side of the street frontage, are all that are left of the terrace of Regency buildings that once stood here.

Beyond the Chestnut paling fence and across the street is the more intact south side of St George's Place and the real subject of the picture. On the left is the Baptist Church of 1860 that can also be seen in the current view below. On the right of the picture are the trees in the walled garden of St George's House, at No. 42 St George's Place. A picture of this impressive red bricked house can be seen on the opposite page.

In the centre of the picture are the old garage premises of Martin Walters Ltd. This firm had taken over a small garage at No. 41 St George's Place, formerly run by Tapleys Motors Ltd. Two other properties between the Baptist Church and the garage had been lost in the blitz.

By the late 1940s Martin Walters had erected two large prefabricated garage buildings on a former garden area, situated behind the cellars of the blitzed properties. These can both be seen in the accompanying picture.

See CAB, Page 42   (Fisk-Moore)

In the early 1950s a more substantial garage showroom building was constructed right on the street frontage. The central part of this new building went up first and took up the site of the old garage forecourt and the garden of St George's House. Then it was extended at either end, first across to the Baptist Chapel and then down to the Regal Cinema. St George's House was demolished to make way for it. However, this was not the end of the destruction. In 1971 four houses nearest the junction with Upper Chantry Lane were pulled down to make way for the Rutland House development.

(Paul Crampton)

The photograph on the right is another of part of the premises of Martin Walters on the south side of the street. In the centre of the picture can be seen two fenced off cellars, once relating to Nos. 39 and 40 St George's Place, both lost in the blitz. To the right of these is a single storey temporary building at No. 41, on the site of Tapley Motors' building, another blitz victim.

At this time Martin Walter operated from a miscellaneous collection of buildings on this site, sandwiched between the Baptist Church and St George's House. Later in the 1950s they would redevelop most of this area in gradual stages.

The right hand turret and porch of the Baptist Church, visible on the left of the picture, were added in 1914 to give the front elevation some symmetry. This was made possible by the demolition of a house. The Baptist Church Hall was built in the same year. In the background and behind the corrugated iron garage buildings can be seen the oast house in Dover Street.

See CAB, Page 42   (Fisk-Moore)

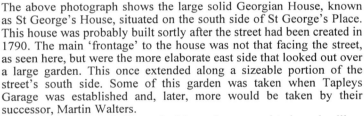

The above photograph shows the large solid Georgian House, known as St George's House, situated on the south side of St George's Place. This house was probably built sortly after the street had been created in 1790. The main 'frontage' to the house was not that facing the street, as seen here, but were the more elaborate east side that looked out over a large garden. This once extended along a sizeable portion of the street's south side. Some of this garden was taken when Tapleys Garage was established and, later, more would be taken by their successor, Martin Walters.

By 1949 St George's House had long since ceased to be a dwelling, or a doctor's surgery as it had been in the 1930s. Now it was the office premises of the Pearl Assurance Company, Arthur Mason Auctioneer and the KCC Planning Department. To the right of the picture can just be seen the edge of the Regal Cinema, surviving today as the Canon.

(Fisk-Moore)

As stated opposite, the south side of St George's Place was more intact than the north side, in fact much more intact! All the pre-war buildings between the Baptist Church and the Upper Chantry Lane junction were standing in the late 1940s. This picture, from January 1949, shows part of the three storey Regency terrace in this section of the street. Sadly, of the three houses in this view, only the one at No. 28 (far left) was still a private residence.

The Holden Plan did not include these buildings in the first development stage. The entire south side was also outside the scope of the Wilson Plan and not subject to any compulsory purchase. However, this did not safeguard any of the buildings from private redevelopment. In the late 1950s St George's House was demolished to expand the premises for Martin Walters. Later still, three houses nearest the Upper Chantry Lane junction, including No. 28, were pulled down for an office development.

(Fisk-Moore)

ST GEORGE'S PLACE (NORTH SIDE)

The few pictures of Canterbury that were taken in the late 1940s were mostly of the same two subjects. One favourite subject was the Cathedral and all the new and uninterrupted views that could be enjoyed since the blitz clearance. The other was any sort of human activity, such as an archaeological investigation or a parade.

The accompanying photograph manages to combine both of these favourite late 1940s subjects. It was taken at the east end of St George's Place in 1948 and shows the Buffs Regiment parading after their freedom of the city ceremony (see also page 34).

The huge vegetation covered void on the north side of St George's Place contributes to the rural feeling that this photograph evokes. The few surviving buildings at the far end, near St George's Crossroads, can also be seen. This picture also has the benefit of a distant but clear view of the towers of the Cathedral from this south-easterly vantage

point. The rest of the Cathedral is hidden by the mature trees still thriving in the rear gardens of the lost houses on the north side of St George's Place.

At this time St George's Place was a single carriageway, albeit a straight and wide one, compared with the majority of thoroughfares in Canterbury. The 1945 Holden Plan for the rebuilding of the city kept it as a single carriageway and retained all the surviving buildings on the north side of the street. This plan was rejected, following the local elections of November 1945. The Wilson Plan that replaced it designated St George's Place as a dual-carriageway, necessitating the removal of these buildings. This, of course, is what ultimately happened.
See CBB, Page 46, BOC, Page 17 – Top, CAB, Page 43 – Top and Bottom (Fisk-Moore)

The Wilson development plan was implemented in 1951. This meant that any new buildings on the north side of St George's Place had to be set well back from the original street frontage, so as to allow for the provision of a second carriageway. The 1950s saw the construction of the new Kentish Gazette offices, as well as the establishment of a large filling station. Nothing more happened until 1969, when the surviving buildings at the far end were demolished to make way for the afore-mentioned second carriageway. Safeways was built in the 1980s.

(Paul Crampton)

In the late 1940s the only standing buildings on the north side of St George's Place could be found at the end nearest St George's Crossroads. The vast majority of the rest of this side was nothing but exposed cellars wherein nature had firmly seized control. The accompanying photograph dates from either 1949 or 1950 and shows a group of the aforementioned surviving buildings. On the left is the tiny shop of Seymour Browne, the watch maker at No. 3 St George's Place. Next to this is the much larger premises of Clark Hunt & Co. Ltd (No. 3a), who dealt in supplies for the building trade. Finally, after the gap, is No. 4, which housed the Isle of Thanet Building Society and several insurance companies. Out of sight to the left is part of the premises of G. Twyman & Son Ltd, situated on the corner with Lower Bridge Street. Pictures of this will appear in future volumes.

(Fisk-Moore)

This wonderful panoramic snow scene was taken from the roof of the old Telephone House on a wintry day in the late 1940s. The East Kent bus, at the crossroads with Upper and Lower Chantry Lane, still wears its wartime livery variation, where battleship grey replaced the cream colour normally applied to the roof. This was done as a camouflage measure against enemy aircraft. Along the north side of St George's Place the thickly fallen snow has settled on the many old cellar and boundary walls to be found here. This makes these ruins very prominent, whereas in the photograph on the opposite page they are hidden beneath summer foliage. Many of the surviving buildings on the street's south side can also clearly be seen on the left of the photograph.

The heavily laden grey sky foretells that there is more snow on the way. The Cathedral, with snow covered roof, dominates the skyline, but its stonework blends into the surrounding greyness.

(Courtesy Mr Peter Jarrett)

This picture shows the Catholic religious procession entering Canterbury, as part of their pilgrimage from Jerusalem. The surviving buildings on the south side of St George's Place can just be seen on the right of this view (see also page 51), although the empty void on the north side is more apparent. However, this section of St George's Place was not completely devoid of buildings. Situated well away from the street frontage and therefore not visible in this picture were the premises of G.H. Denne & Son Ltd, building contractors. In the centre of the view and further from the camera can be seen the headquarters building of the British Legion at No. 7 New Dover Road.

The Holden Plan sited the bus and coach station on this large overgrown area north of St George's Place. Hugh Wilson sited his bus station in St George's Lane and the coach station in St Peter's Lane, both within the line of the city walls.

See CBB, Page 47 – Top and BOC, Page 16 – Bottom
(Fisk-Moore)

LADY WOOTTONS GREEN

The houses on both sides of Lady Woottons Green were all badly damaged by bomb blast in the June 1942 blitz. Subsequently, all but one of these were demolished in the latter half of 1942 and in 1943.

The sole survivor, a large Georgian House at No. 1 Lady Woottons Green, can be seen on the right of the picture. Behind the house and adjoining it can be seen a flint wall. The better constructed section nearest the house is part of the ruin of the former St Augustine's Almonry Chapel. What appears to be a small lancet window is visible in the west facing wall. Furthermore, in the south facing wall, almost hidden by the holly tree, can just be seen a low and blocked Gothic doorway. The rest of the long west wall is made from brick and ecclesiastical demolition material, no doubt recovered from ruinous buildings once associated with St Augustine's Abbey.

The empty site in the foreground, on the corner of Broad Street and the north side of Lady Woottons Green, was once occupied by a large post-medieval house called 'The Priory'. In the late 1940s, when this picture was taken, no trace of it could be found, apart from a cellar on the Broad Street frontage.

The 3-D model of the 1945 Holden Plan showed Lady Woottons Green kept very much as it was in the post blitz period, i.e. with the one blitz-surviving house retained. It also showed the central green area and the empty bomb sites either side of the house planted out with trees.

The superceding Wilson Plan was unspecific about this area, but showed nearby Monastery Street extended from Lady Woottons Green through to Havelock Street.

See CBB, Page 54 and CAB, Page 51 – Upper Left (Fisk-Moore)

The empty corner site, prominent in the picture, was finally redeveloped in 1955, with the construction of Diocesan House. This was the first new post-war building to appear in Lady Woottons Green. The terrace of Georgian style houses on the opposite side of the green was built in the late 1950s. The old flint wall behind the 18th century house still exists, but has been almost entirely rebuilt. Sadly, none of the above mentioned architectural features have survived. Recently, Diocesan House received a very imaginative rear extension.

(Paul Crampton)

These pictures show the Findon Gate in the late 1940s, before and after restoration. The one on the left dates from 1946 and features the gate and surrounding buildings, still showing the scars of the blitz. The stone facing around the lower half of the left tower had been blasted clean away. The wooden shoring was replaced here in 1942, to await the time when repair work could be carried out.

The right hand photograph, from June 1948, was taken when restoration work to all of the old former St Augustine's Abbey buildings was nearing completion. The new stone facing can clearly be seen on the Findon Gate. Today the different stone used has not weathered in and the 1947/1948 repair work is still obvious.
See TAN, Page 7 – Top Right and CAB, Page 47 – Bottom   (Fisk-Moore)

This wonderful 1946 photograph has been reproduced as large as possible, so that its many details can be more fully appreciated. It was taken from the top of the old Cemetery Gate and looks along Church Street St Pauls, across Broad Street and into the tree-filled Cathedral Precincts. The effects of the blitz are still apparent and the surviving buildings have that drab appearance, typical of the early post-war years. A number of interesting buildings can be seen along the east side of Broad Street, opposite the car park and city wall. Many of these, particularly those away from the street frontage, can no longer be found.

See CBB, Page 50 (Fisk-Moore)

Throughout the 1960s and early 1970s the attrition in Burgate Lane continued. Buildings on both sides were pulled down piecemeal as they became vacant, which gave the lane a rather shabby and derelict appearance. The last of the doomed houses to survive were the three storey ones, seen in the middle distance in the old photograph. They too finally disappeared in 1974, to make way for the large shopping development seen in this current view. Today Zoar Chapel still survives, as do the two buildings nearest the camera.

(Paul Crampton)

BURGATE LANE AND BURGATE STREET (EAST SECTION)

Burgate Lane survived the Canterbury blitz relatively intact and lost only a few buildings at the St George's Street end. Just how intact it was can be seen in the accompanying photograph, taken from the Burgate Street end in 1949. This fascinating jumble of buildings date from the 16th to the 19th centuries. The most interesting of these can be seen at the far (St George's Street) end of the lane, in the form of a row of cottages constructed largely of Caen Stone blocks. The materials had been purchased and recovered from the ruins of St Augustine's Abbey Church in the year immediately after the dissolution.

The post war Holden Plan of 1945 would have cleared Burgate Lane of all old buildings except for Zoar Chapel (which is just out of sight in this view). This was replaced by the Wilson Plan, conceived in 1947 and implemented in 1951. The latter approved plan retained all buildings on the right of the picture, up to and including the white rendered houses. However, it planned to do away with the Caen Stone houses and all of the buildings against the city wall, on the left of the photograph, except again for Zoar Chapel which is built into the city wall.

During the 1940s Burgate Lane was left alone. In fact, one could stroll down this undulating lane almost unaware that most of the rest of the St George's parish had disappeared. Then, in the 1950s, the Caen Stone cottages were demolished as planned, but so were the white rendered houses that were to have been retained. At the same time, a new shop was constructed in the gap, seen in the foreground on the right.

See TAN, Page 10 and Page 29

(Alan Stingemore)

The Roman Catholic religious procession is once more featured in this view of the east end of Burgate Street. In the background can be seen part of the premises of Invicta Motors, as discussed on page 47. However, what is of more interest is the Saracens Head public house, which provides a backdrop for the crucifix-carrying pilgrims. This fine 17th century quadruple gabled building was constructed just outside the city walls, at a time when the Burgate City Gate was still standing.

The Saracens Head stood at a point where the wide Broad Street narrowed considerably to become Lower Bridge Street. This was to be the route of the ring road, whichever development plan was to be implemented. Therefore, the pub was doomed from 1945 onwards, but managed to hang on until being finally demolished in 1969. Timbers from the Saracens Head were then used in Anthony Swaine's restoration of Eastbridge Hospital (see page 9). *See TAN, Pages 38 and 45 – Top* (Fisk-Moore)

This photograph certainly looks like one with a story behind it. Unfortunately, I do not know what it is! The picture features the south-east corner of St Thomas' Roman Catholic Church and was taken from Canterbury Lane. The firemen, searching along the parapet, give the impression that this is a wartime view. However, the undated negative was of the type used by Fisk-Moore in the late 1940s. Moreover, the overgrown vegetation round the base of the church would suggest a late 1940s date. At this time the church building was something of a landmark, being clearly visible from the empty St George's Street. It was also a prominent feature in Burgate Street, where so many buildings on the south side had perished.

Canterbury Lane, just to the east of St Thomas' Church, contained some blitz surviving buildings that could still be found in the late 1940s. Much of the former St George's Primary School still stood on the lane's east side. So did Loyns Bakery, which could be found further south and near to the ruins of St George's Church.

(Fisk-Moore)

We are now looking at the front of St Thomas' Church, as viewed from Burgate Street. It was designed in a gothic style by Canterbury architect John Green Hall and dates from 1874 and 1875. The church is situated on land immediately behind the site of the redundant Anglican church of St Mary Magdalene. All but the church's tower, visible on the right, had been demolished a few years before the new church emerged.

St Thomas' was a lucky survivor of the 1942 blitz, but did sustain minor blast damage to the windows and pinnacle on the Burgate Street frontage. The accompanying photograph was taken in about 1949 or 1950, just after repair work had been carried out. The picture clearly shows the attractive symmetrical lines of John Green Hall's design, emphasised here by the uncluttered background. Sadly, this was spoilt in 1962 by the addition of hideous concrete extensions to either side of the church.

(Fisk-Moore)

BURGATE STREET (NORTH-EAST)

As a result of the blitz of Canterbury, two large voids could be found on the north side of Burgate Street. The one in the middle section of the street, caused by the four-ton bomb, attracted many photographers as it offered a wonderful view of almost all of the Cathedral. The photograph on page 62 is a fine example of this. The void at the eastern end of Burgate Street was rarely photographed in the late 1940s except here, in 1948, as the backdrop to a parade.

These gentlemen are from St Augustine's College and are marching to the Cathedral as part of their centenary festival. The photographer, Mr W. Fisk-Moore, has not travelled too far to take this picture. His studio can be seen on the other side of the street to the left. Fisk-Moore came here after their previous shop and studio were lost in the bombing. Their current premises at No. 10c Burgate Street were constructed in 1931, as an in-fill development, on a former garden area between two existing buildings. This shop was damaged in 1942, as can be seen by the presence of a temporary corrugated iron roof.

Next to Fisk-Moore's shop, Starrs House once stood on much of the empty space, of which more is mentioned on the page opposite. The mature trees seen in the picture are standing in the garden of the lost Starrs House.

The rest of the void was occupied by a terrace of small houses and shops numbered 5 to 9 Burgate Street. A surviving pair of cottages at Nos. 3 and 4 are visible at the far end. They are still there today at the end of Burgate Street, now simply called 'Burgate'. Furthest from the camera can be seen the three storey buildings on the corner of Lower Bridge Street and Church Street St Paul's (see also page 47).

See BOC, Page 13 – Top and Page 34 – Middle   (Fisk-Moore)

The entire site was redeveloped in the early 1950s, with modern shops built in an older style. In fact, all the new shops on the north side of Burgate Street (i.e. under the auspices of the Dean and Chapter) were built in more traditional styles, or gave the appearance of being so. In the very late 1940s many trees were felled on the area of land between the South Precincts and the north of Burgate Street. The old trees in the above picture disappeared at this time. The Fisk-Moore shop was later repaired and given a new roof.

(Paul Crampton)

As is mentioned opposite, just to the east of the Fisk-Moore shop could be found the site of Starrs House. This was a large Georgian House, owned by the Dean and Chapter and a victim of the blitz. Starrs House was numbered either 14d The Precincts or 10a Burgate Street, depending on what side of it you were standing. In the late 1940s all that remained of the house was a large cellar and a section of the west wall, adjacent to the Fisk-Moore shop. To the side and rear of the cellar large trees continued to thrive in the untended garden area.

The accompanying picture dates from early 1949 and shows the aforementioned cellar, complete with tree saplings and shrubs. Inevitably, Buddleia is the dominant species, but a Willow sapling has also taken hold. This well composed photograph, so typical of the period, is finished off beautifully by the Bell Harry Tower looming up over the scene.

See BOC, Page 13 – Top and Page 34 – Middle   (Fisk-Moore)

This picture shows the tail end of the aforementioned Catholic procession, as it turned into St Thomas' Church on the south side of Burgate Street. Also featured are a number of interesting and familiar buildings on the left, or north side of the street. Furthest from the camera is the Fisk-Moore shop, more clearly visible on the opposite page. Next is the large three storey and smaller two storey building that comprise The Little Café at Nos. 11, 11b and 12 Burgate Street. The proprietor, Miss Laura Barrow, proudly advertised that everything served was home made.

(Fisk-Moore)

Properties on the north side of Burgate Street back straight on to the South Precincts of the Cathedral, although many do have small back garden areas. In places along the north-east section of the street the precincts boundary came within a few yards of the street frontage. In the late 1940s many mature trees could be found all over this area. A number of them, particularly those in the garden area immediately behind the site of Starrs House, had become very large indeed. Others still showed signs of the blast damage suffered in the 1942 blitz.

In 1949 the Dean and Chapter decided to clear away a number of these trees. The accompanying picture shows local contractors, Charles Hewitt Ltd, engaged in this process. The cull was, in part, to free areas of the South Precincts for redevelopment in the next year. This would include a large new house, built on the site of Canon Macnutt's residence lost in the blitz. Rows of new shops would also be built in the gaps along the north Burgate Street frontage.

(Fisk-Moore)

IRON BAR LANE AND BURGATE STREET
(SOUTH-WEST SECTION)

Iron Bar Lane, the middle one of five connecting lanes between Burgate Street and Canterbury's main street, was the worst affected by the blitz of 1942. In the late 1940s the lane passed across a vast open space covered in vegetation, where once were crowded a miscellany of buildings on both sides. The only standing structures to be found were two small garage buildings that had somehow managed to survive the bombing and later clearance operations.

The accompanying old photograph was taken in about 1949 and features the end of the lane nearest Burgate Street. In the years between the blitz and the reconstruction the empty bomb sites on both sides of the lane had become a temporary car park. A number of cars from the period can be seen in the foreground.

On the left can be seen one of the aforementioned garages, built in the pre-war years, probably the 1930s. The adjoining wall on the lane's west side is contemporary with the garage. Behind the garage wall are two surviving buildings on the north side of Burgate Street (see page 63). Of particular interest is the small medieval cottage on the right.

Archaeological investigations were carried out along Iron Bar Lane in the late 1940s, but these were confined mainly to the cellars at either end, adjacent to Burgate and St George's Street. Photographs, as well as more information about these digs, can be found on the page opposite.

See CBB, Page 58 and CAB, Page 56

(Courtesy Canterbury Archaeological Trust)

Iron Bar Lane had always been too narrow for motor vehicles at the St George's Street end. This restriction was continued when the lane was re-modelled in the spring of 1952. At this time a square car park was constructed in the middle of the lane and the northern section leading into Burgate Street widened. A new link lane imaginatively called 'Link Lane' was also constructed between the new square car park and nearby Canterbury Lane. The block of shops in the centre of the current view was constructed along the widened section of Iron Bar Lane in the late 1950s.

(Paul Crampton)

Near to the St George's Street junction Iron Bar Lane was at its narrowest. In the late 1940s cellars fell away on either side and were fenced off for safety. This gave the impression of crossing a bridge or causeway when entering the narrow section of the lane from the main street. The accompanying picture was taken from St George's Street in April 1949 and looks north along Iron Bar Lane. In the foreground is the cellar of No. 19 St George's Street, once the premises of the tailors, Wilson & Waller Ltd. The rear wall of the cellar, including an interesting round topped arch, is visible in the foreground.

Behind and to the right of the cellar can just be seen three volunteer archaeologists, hard at work. They are digging a trench, much of which is situated in the small former garden area behind the site of the tailor's shop. This trench unearthed no Roman structures, but brought to light a medieval well and some wall foundations from the same period.

(Courtesy Canterbury Archaeological Trust)

This photograph was taken much further along the east side of Iron Bar Lane and near to its junction with Burgate Street. On the left can be seen the St Mary Magdalene tower and to the right the Roman Catholic St Thomas' Church (see also page 57). The cars in the foreground are parked on a blitzed site, once occupied by some medieval cottages and a large brick warehouse.

The first stage of the Holden Plan was quite specific about this area. Iron Bar Lane was to become a service road from Burgate Street leading to a service yard and small car park. The St George's Street end was to be completely sealed off by new buildings fronting the main street. A plan of the area between Iron Bar Lane and Canterbury Lane as redeveloped under the Holden Plan was included in a booklet published by Canterbury City Council in 1945. The plan was compared with another, showing the area redeveloped on a freehold basis, as the CCDA wanted it.

See CBB, Page 58 and BOC, Page 44 – Top Left   (Alan Stingemore)

Further archaeological investigations were carried out in cellars along the south side of Burgate Street, in the section west of Iron Bar Lane. In the third quarter of the 19th century some Roman mosaics had been found in this vicinity, so there was a high expectation of further important finds. On the western corner of the Iron Bar Lane junction were two open cellars that used to be beneath two fine post-medieval timber framed buildings at Nos. 55 and 56 Burgate Street. In about 1948 a trench was sunk in each of them. These revealed two rooms of a Roman house and many contemporary coins. A third larger trench was dug in the former garden area behind the site of No. 55. This is the trench featured in the accompanying photograph. A bakehouse must have once stood here, because the excavation yielded a sequence of three pitched tile ovens. These were thought to date from the 14th century. In the picture, a representative from the Canterbury Excavation Committee is showing the ovens to keen onlookers, who may be members of the Canterbury Archaeological Society.

See BOC, Page 9 – Left and CAB, Page 57 – Top

(Courtesy Canterbury Archaeological Trust)

BURGATE STREET (NORTH-WEST SECTION)

In the eight years from June 1942 until autumn 1950 both residents of and visitors to Canterbury could not fail to have been shocked by the destruction caused by the blitz and its aftermath. However, many if not all were equally awestruck by the wonderful views of the Cathedral that could now be enjoyed from the flattened central area.

No view of Canterbury Cathedral was more spectacular than from Burgate Street where almost its entire length could be appreciated. This large void on the north side of the street had been caused by the four-ton bomb, targetted on the Cathedral, but missing narrowly. This amazing view is reproduced in the accompanying photograph, taken in January 1949. The Kent Co-operative Society Funeral Service have chosen this as a backdrop for their immaculate but sombre looking vehicles.

The large bomb crater had long since been filled in with demolition rubble brought in from the bombsites all around and was now becoming overgrown. Many surviving trees in the South Precincts can be seen around the site of the crater. The large Beech tree on the extreme right is standing atop the Campanile Mound, where once stood a medieval bell tower. Each year, in late winter and early spring, the mound would be covered by thousands of snowdrops.

The Cathedral itself appears very much as it had throughout the 1940s, with plain glass and wooden blanks in most of the windows. The ancient and irreplaceable stained glass was still in storage at this time, even though the war had been over more than three years. The windows would be restored in the early 1950s.

See CAB, Page 54 (Fisk-Moore)

The new arcade of shops built across the central gap was the first new permanent construction to appear in post-war Canterbury. This enterprise was funded in the greater part by the Canadian Government. The shops reflect a traditional architectural style, although they are built round a steel frame. This method of construction usually means a life-span of only 100 years. So perhaps in the year 2050, when this development is demolished, archaeologists will excavate the old bomb crater. What fascinating fragments of the many blitzed Canterbury buildings dumped here will then be discovered!

(Paul Crampton)

Originally I could not decide which of the available photographs of the bomb crater area to use, this one or the one on page 62. In the end, I included them both. This picture was taken with a wider angled lens, which has meant that all of Bell Harry Tower can be seen. The Beech trees with full summer foliage contrast well with their bleak wintry appearance on the opposite page.

The strip of land along the north of Burgate Street at this location was to be compulsorily purchased from the Dean and Chapter, according to the 1945 Holden Plan. The 1947 Wilson Plan considerably reduced the amount of compulsory purchase and did not include this area.

In August 1948 four archaeological trenches were dug along the western edge of this site. There was no point in excavating anywhere else, because the bomb crater eliminated all archaeological levels and was now full of demolition rubble. In any case, the small area that was investigated turned up nothing of worth.

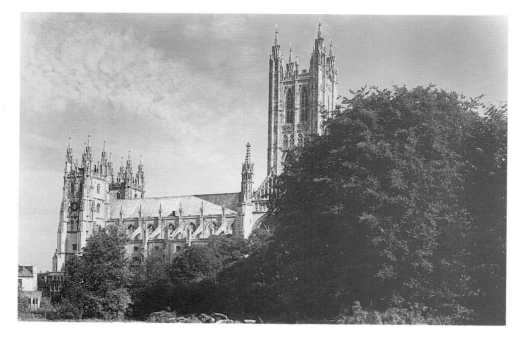

See CAB, Page 55 – Top   (Fisk-Moore)

To the west of the bomb crater is a fine collection of buildings on the north side of the street. Most of these had escaped the worst of the blitz and, in the late 1940s, only the one immediately next to the crater still showed scars of the blitz. This was a small two storey late medieval house at No. 23 Burgate Street, last occupied by Miss E. Norris, who had a small toy shop on the ground floor. The shop was blitz damaged and remained empty for the rest of the 1940s. Its scorched frontage appears on the right of the accompanying picture, but the whole shop can better be seen on page 60.

The photograph is dominated by the premises of Court Brothers (Furnishers) Ltd, at No. 24 Burgate Street. Also visible to the left is the builders merchants shop of Alfred Oldby at No. 25.

Having survived the 1940s against all odds, the little medieval building was demolished in early 1950 by the Dean and Chapter, just prior to the redevelopment of the site (see below).

See CBB, Page 57 – Middle   (Fisk-Moore)

This final picture dates from August 1950 and shows the start of the construction of a row of new shops that would close up the gap and once more hide the Cathedral away in its precincts. This was the first new permanent building in post-war Canterbury. It heralded a new era for the city and also marked the end of the 'Buddleia Years'. This Dean and Chapter building project was largely financed by the Canadian Government.

The Wilson Plan (which did not include this development) was implemented in 1951 and the major reconstruction of Canterbury began later that year in St George's Street. The overgrown south side of Burgate Street, seen in the foreground of the accompanying picture, would not be built upon until 1958.

The early 1950s was an interesting time in Canterbury. New buildings began to mushroom all over the blitzed areas of the city and old ones continued to disappear. In fact, I feel another book coming on!

(Courtesy Canterbury Archaeological Trust)

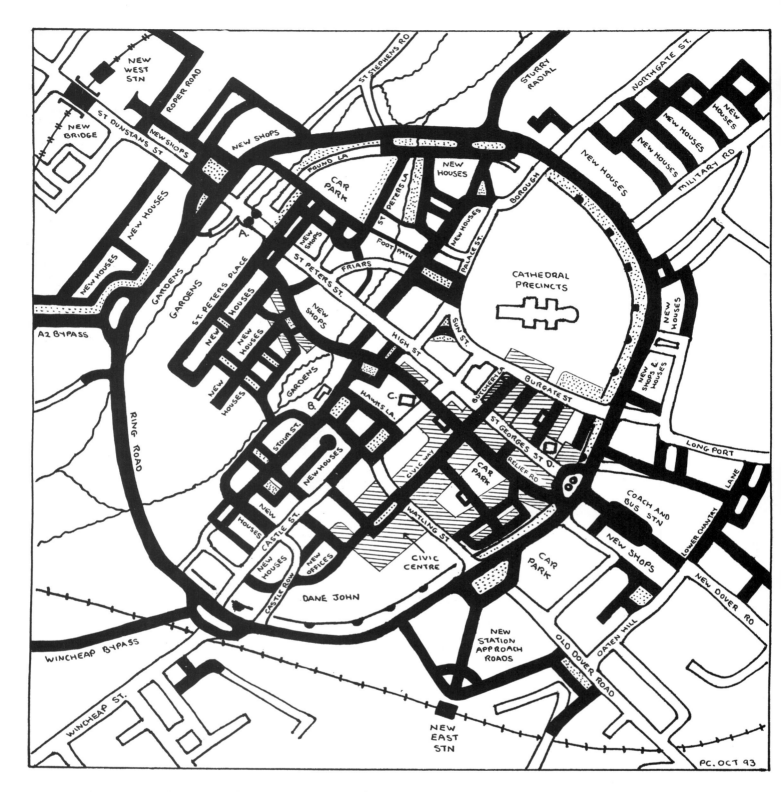

HOLDEN PLAN - COMPLETED VERSION
Comprehensive redevelopment of the whole city

☐ : Existing roads unchanged.

■ : New roads (or existing roads widened).

▨ : New buildings (First stage only).

▦ : New open spaces.

┿┿┿ : New railway route.

Points of reference :

A – Westgate.

B – Poor Priests Hospital.

C – St Margarets Church.

D – St Georges Church (Complete shell retained).

THE HOLDEN PLAN – COMPLETED VERSION